C000102906

AQA A Level Physics

Turning Points in Physics

Dr Asad Altimeemy

Preface

This book is aimed specifically at the AQA A level Physics Option Unit, Turning Points in Physics. The book covers all the requirement of this unit. This option unit is intended to enable key concepts and developments in Physics to be studied in greater depth than in the core content. Students will be able to appreciate Physics from historical and conceptual viewpoints. Many present-day technological industries are the consequence of these key developments. The topics in the option illustrate how unforeseen technologies can develop from new discoveries. The book contains over 50 worked Questions. Questions are included at relevant points in the text so that students can obtain an immediate test of their understanding of a topic. I have added more than 50 revision questions at the end of the book.

Dr Asad Altimeemy
BSc PhD PGCE MInstP
February 2020

Copyright © 2019 Author Dr Asad Altimeemy
All rights reserved.
ISBN: 9781795472883

Dedicated to Caroline and Adnan

CONTENTS

Chapter 1

Cathode Rays

Dry air is a bad conductor to electricity. However, under certain conductions, electric current is found to flow through a gas. For instance, at the time of lightning, very high electric current passes through the air for a short duration. The conduction of electricity through gases at low pressures was investigated extensively for much of the latter half of the nineteenth century, following Johann Geissler's invention of an improved vacuum pump in 1855. These investigations led ultimately to the discovery of the electron.

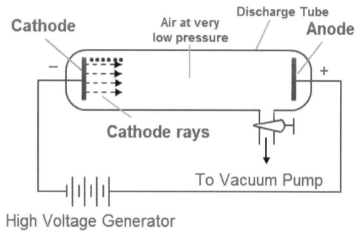

Figure 1.1 Cathode ray tube circuit diagram

When the gas pressure inside Cathode ray tube is equal to atmospheric pressure, a very high electric field of the order of 30,000 volts or higher is necessary to produce an electric discharge through the gas. In this case, a luminous electric spark is found to be produced between the electrodes from time to time attended with sharp crackling sound. This is known as a spark discharge which proceeds along narrow and zig-zag paths. The sparks are momentary and repetitive. The different sparks proceed along different paths.

1

When the gas pressure is reduced, the potential difference required to produce the sparks becomes less. However, when the pressure is very low, it becomes difficult to initiate a discharge through the gas. The colour of the glow depends on the nature of the gas, its pressure and the PD across the tube. No glow discharge appears in the tube unless the gas pressure is below 10 mm of Hg. Remember atmospheric pressure is 750 mm Hg.

Just below that pressure, a glow appears as a bright blue streamer, flickering back and forth between the two electrodes, attended with repeated crackling sound. As the pressure is reduced to about 0.5 mm of mercury, there is a stable discharge in the tube and a buzzing sound is heard. A pale purple luminous discharge, which broadens sidewise, spreads through the entire region between the cathode and the anode.

As the gas pressure is reduced further, the negative glow is detached from the cathode and moves away from it towards the anode producing a new, dark space between it and the cathode, known as the Crooke's dark space. Furthermore, under this condition, another luminous region known as the cathode glow, appears at the cathode. During all these changes, the colours of the different luminous regions change.

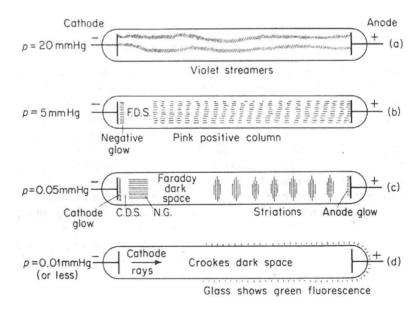

Figure 1.2 Cathode ray under different pressure

2

At a low enough pressure, a pink glow fills the entire tube. Continued decreases in pressure causes the pink glow to concentrate around the anode and a blue glow around the cathode. The space between the glows is dark and called Faraday's dark space.

If the pressure is reduced below about 0.01mmHg, the glow largely disappears and parts of the wall of the tube start to fluoresce. The colour of this fluorescence depends on the impurities present in the glass; it does not depend on the gas in the tube.

Careful observations have shown that a stream of high velocity charged particles is emitted from the cathode which falls on the anode as well as on the walls of the glass tube. As a result of this impact, the walls of the tube emit bluish or greenish fluorescent radiation. The streams of the particles emitted from the cathode are known as cathode-rays.

Cathode rays behave as if they are negatively charged particles.

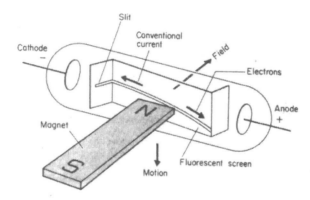

Figure 1.3a Deflection of cathode ray by magnetic field

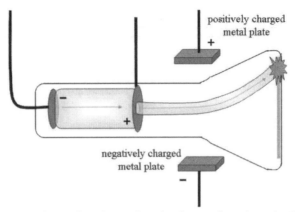

Figure 1.3b Deflection of cathode ray by electric field

Properties of Cathode rays

They are produced by the negative electrode, or cathode, in an evacuated tube, and travel towards the anode.
They cause fluorescence.
They emitted at 90° to the surface of the cathode
They travel in straight lines and cast sharp shadows.
They are deflected by electric and magnetic fields and have a negative charge.
They are beams of tiny, negatively charged particles called electrons.
They can be focused using a concave cathode
They are produced by a heating effect
They blacken photographic plates.
They pass through thin metal foil without puncturing them.
They could produce X rays if they had sufficiently high energy

Thermionic Emission

Metals contain many free electrons moving at high speed and at random between the atoms of the material. If these free electrons are given enough energy, they may escape from the metal surface.

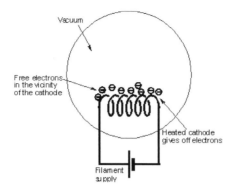

Figure 1.4 Thermionic emission

One way to give the free electrons sufficient energy to allow them to escape is to heat the metal. The emission of free electrons from a 'hot' metal surface is called Thermionic Emission.

If we put a negative plate in front of hot metal, any electrons that are emitted will be pushed back towards the metal by the negative charge on the plate. None of them will get far from the metal. This happens because the electrons are also negatively charged.

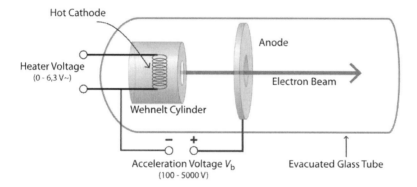

Figure 1.5 Electron gun

If the potential difference between the cathode and the anode is V, the mass of the electron (m) and the charge on the electron (e) the velocity with which the electrons emerge from the electron gun is given by:

$$Electron\ velocity, v = \sqrt{\frac{2eV}{m}} \quad ---(1.1)$$

You could derive the above equation from the conservation of energy.

The energy absorbed by electrons from the pd V (work done) = eV

$$eV = \frac{1}{2}mv^2$$

rearrange

$$\frac{2eV}{m} = v^2$$

and square root

$$v = \sqrt{\frac{2eV}{m}}$$

Thomson's Tube

Thomson's experiments established that cathode rays are made up of a beam of negatively charged particles. Due to the very large potential difference applied between the two electrodes in the discharge tube, they acquire very high kinetic energy in travelling from the cathode to the anode. As a result, they travel with very high velocity inside the discharge tube. It has been found that irrespective of the nature of the gas present in the tube, these negatively charged particles have always the same properties. This shows that they are universal constituents of all matter. These have since been named electrons, a name originally coined by Johnstone Stoney during his studies on electrolytic conduction.

Since all substances are made up of atoms and since the electrons are present in all substances, we may conclude that they must be present within the atoms of all substances. Since the atoms are electrically neutral, the atoms must therefore be made up of two parts, one of which carries positive electricity while the other an equal amount of negative electricity.

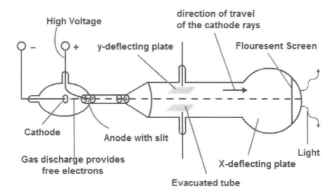

High Voltage

direction of travel
of the cathode rays

y-deflecting plate

Flouresent Screen

Cathode

Anode with slit

Gas discharge provides
free electrons

X-deflecting plate

Light

Evacuated tube

Figure 1.6 Thomson tube diagram

By adjusting the relative strength of the electric and magnetic fields, the particles went straight.

The electric force on the negative charge is equal to magnetic force

$$F_E = qE \ --- (1.2)$$

Where q is the charge of the cathode ray particle and E is the electric field strength.

Using Fleming's left-hand rule, the magnetic force is down, and it is equal to $F_m = qvB$

Where v is speed of the cathode ray particle and B is magnetic field strength.

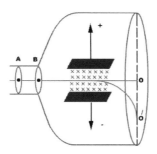

Figure 1.7 Deflection of electron beam by electric and magnetic fields

If $F_E = F_m$

$$eE = evB$$

Where e is the charge of electron

From the above equation

$$v = \frac{E}{B}$$

Using

$$v = \sqrt{\frac{2eV}{m}}$$

$$\frac{E}{B} = \sqrt{\frac{2eV}{m}}$$

$$\frac{V}{Bd} = \sqrt{\frac{2eV}{m}}$$

$$\frac{e}{m} = \frac{V}{2d^2B^2} \ - - - (1.3)$$

Where V is the PD between the horizontal plates and d is the distance between them. Another method is to use electric fields deflection.

Using Newton's second law of motion for constant mass, $F = ma$

$$eE = ma \ - - - (1.4)$$

To use the equation above, we need find the value of acceleration, a

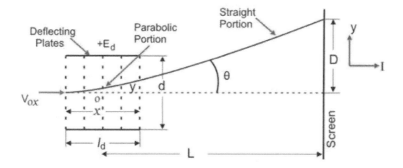

Figure 1.8 Measure speed of electron from deflection

Looking at the diagram above, the deflection D is the result of the acceleration due to electric fields.

Using

$$s = ut + \frac{1}{2}at^2$$

For vertical motion

$$y = 0 + \frac{1}{2}\frac{eE}{m}t^2$$

Where y is the deflection as the charge particle leaves the plates and the electric fields influence decrease to zero.

$$y = \frac{1}{2}\frac{eE}{m}t^2 \quad ---(1.5)$$

For horizontal motion $x = vt$

$$t = \frac{x}{v}$$

The equation of trajectory of the electron:

$$y = \frac{1}{2}\frac{eEx^2}{mv^2}$$

9

$$\frac{dy}{dx} = \frac{eEx}{mv^2}$$

Where l is the length of the plates.

$$\frac{dy}{dx} = \frac{eEl}{mv^2}$$

$$\frac{dy}{dx} = \frac{D}{L}$$

$$\frac{eEl}{mv^2} = \frac{D}{L}$$

$$\frac{e}{m} = \frac{Dv^2}{ElL}$$

Using

$$v = \frac{E}{B}$$

$$\frac{e}{m} = \frac{DE}{B^2 lL} \ - - - - (1.6)$$

D, L, l, E and B are easy to measure.

From measurements and equations for deflecting particles by magnetic and electric fields, the charge to mass ratio was determined (1.76×10^{11} C/kg).

The charge to mass ratio (e/m) was the same regardless of the potential difference used to accelerate particles. This e/m was the same for different cathode materials. It indicates that there must be a similarity between particles making up different cathode materials.

Similar experiments with hydrogen ions showed that the hydrogen ion's charge to mass ratio was 1836 times smaller than for cathode rays. If we assumed that equal charges were present on the hydrogen ions and cathode ray particles, then the mass of the cathode ray particles was 1/1836 of the mass for the hydrogen ion.

10

Thomson concluded that cathode rays were light, fast moving, negative particles that were a part of an atom.

Motion in magnetic field

If the magnetic field is perpendicular to the velocity of the electron, then path of the electron is circular.

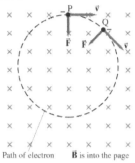

Figure 1.9 Electron deflection by magnetic fields

$$magnetic\ force = Bev = \frac{mv^2}{r}$$

$$v = \frac{Ber}{m} \ - - - (1.7)$$

and $\ r = \frac{mv}{Be} \ - - - (1.8)$

If the electron enters the field at an angle to the field direction, the resulting path of the electron will be helical as shown in figure 1.10. Such motion occurs above the poles of the earth where charges particles from the Sun spiral through the Earth's field to produce the aurorae.

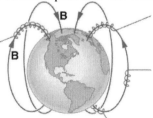

Figure 1.10 Charged particles tripped by Earth's magnetic field

Examples

1. Calculate the speed of an electron which has been acceleration from rest through a PD of 10 V.

$$eV = \frac{1}{2}mv^2$$

$$v = \sqrt{\frac{2eV}{m}} = \sqrt{\frac{2 \times 10 \times 1.6 \times 10^{-19}}{9.1 \times 10^{-31}}} = 1875228.9 \ m/s$$

2. An electron moves from A to B. Its speed at A is 2×10^6 m/s. Calculate its speed on reaching B,

If B is 4V positive relative to A

$$eV = \frac{1}{2}mv^2$$

$$v = \sqrt{\frac{2eV}{m}} = \sqrt{\frac{2 \times 4 \times 1.6 \times 10^{-19}}{9.1 \times 10^{-31}}} = 1185998.9 \ m/s$$

final velocity $= 2 \times 10^6 + 1185998.9 = 3185998.9$

b) If B is 4V negative relative to A

$$eV = \frac{1}{2}mv^2$$

$$v = \sqrt{\frac{2eV}{m}} = \sqrt{\frac{2 \times 4 \times 1.6 \times 10^{-19}}{9.1 \times 10^{-31}}} = 1185998.9 \ m/s$$

final velocity $= 2 \times 10^6$ - $1185998.9 = 814001$ m/s

3. A beam of electrons is acceleration through a PD of 600 V and then enters a uniform electric field of strength 5×10^3 V/m created by two parallel plates each of length 2×10^{-2} m. Calculate:

The speed, v, of the electrons as they enter the field

$$v = \sqrt{\frac{2eV}{m}}$$

$$v = \sqrt{\frac{2 \times 600 \times 1.6 \times 10^{-19}}{9.1 \times 10^{-31}}} = 14525460.8 \; m/s$$

The time, t, that each electron spends in the field

$$t = \frac{x}{v} = \frac{0.02}{14525460.8} = 1.37 \times 10^{-9} \; s$$

The angle, θ, through which the electrons have been deflected by the electrons have been deflected by the time they emerge from the field

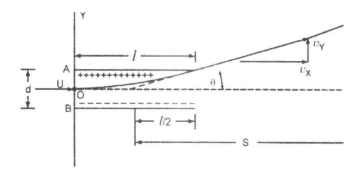

$$v_y = u_y + a_y t$$

$$v_y = 0 + \frac{eE}{m}t$$

$$v_y = \frac{1.6 \times 10^{-19} \times 5 \times 10^3}{9.1 \times 10^{-31}} \times 1.37 \times 10^{-9}$$

$$= 1204395.6$$

$$\theta = tan^{-1}\frac{v_y}{v_x} = tan^{-1}\frac{1204395.6}{14525460.8} = 4.7^o$$

13

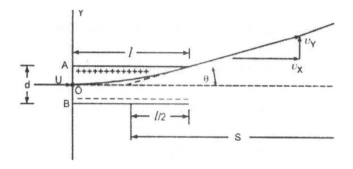

4. An electron moving horizontally at 2×10^5 m/s enters a uniform electric field which is directly vertically downwards and has a strength of 90 V/m. The electron leaves the field 3×10^{-8} s later with speed v. find v

There will be no change in velocity in horizontal direction

$$F = ma = eE$$

$$a = \frac{e}{m}E$$

Using $v = u + at$

$$v_y = a_y t = \frac{e}{m}E\,t$$

$$v_y = \frac{1.6 \times 10^{-19}}{9.1 \times 10^{-31}} \times 90 \times 3 \times 10^{-8} = 474725 \; m/s$$

$$v = \sqrt{v_x^2 + v_y^2} = 515135 \; m/s$$

$$\theta = tan^{-1}\frac{v_y}{v_x} = 67.15°$$

5. An electron is moving in a circular path at 5×10^6 m/s in a uniform magnetic field of a flex density 3×10^{-4} T. Find the radius of the path.

$$evB = \frac{mv^2}{r}$$

$$r = \frac{mv}{eB} = 0.095 \; m$$

6. An electron moving horizontally at 3×10^6 m/s enters a uniform electric field of 400 V/m which directly vertically down wards. The electron travels a horizontal distance of 10 cm whilst in the field. Find

a) the time for which electron is in the field

$$t = \frac{d}{v} = \frac{0.01}{3 \times 10^6} = 3.33 \times 10^{-9} \; s$$

b) its vertical component of acceleration in the field

$$F = ma = eE$$

$$a = \frac{e}{m} E = \frac{1.6 \times 10^{-19}}{9.1 \times 10^{-31}} \times 400 = 7 \times 10^{13} \; m/s^2$$

c) the amount by which it is displaced vertically, and

$$\text{using } s = ut + 0.5 \times at^2 = 3.88 \times 10^{-4} \; m$$

d) the speed with which it emerges from the field.

$$\text{Using } y = u + at = 0 + 7 \times 10^{13} \times 3.33 \times 10^{-9}$$

$$y = 2.33 \times 10^5 \; m$$

$$v = \sqrt{v_x^2 + v_y^2} = 3009042 \; m/s$$

$$\theta = tan^{-1} \frac{v_y}{v_x} = 4.44°$$

7. An electron is accelerated from rest through a PD of 80 V. It then enters a uniform magnetic field of flux density 6×10^{-4} T and starts to travel along a circular path. Find the radius of the path.

$$eV = \frac{1}{2}mv^2$$

$$v = \sqrt{\frac{2eV}{m}}$$

$$v = \sqrt{\frac{2 \times 1.6 \times 10^{-19} \times 80}{9.1 \times 10^{-31}}} = 5303948 \, m/s$$

$$evB = \frac{mv^2}{r}$$

$$r = \frac{mv}{eB} = 0.05 \, m$$

8. An oil drop with a mass of 1.2×10^{-15} kg is held stationary between two parallel metal plates whose separation is 6 mm. The drop carries a charge of 4.8×10^{-19} C. Ignoring the up thrust due to air, calculate:

The electric field strength between the plates
$$qE = mg$$

$$E = \frac{mg}{q} = \frac{1.2 \times 10^{-15} \times 9.81}{4.8 \times 10^{-19}} = 24525 \, V/m$$

The PD across the plates
$$E = \frac{V}{d}$$

$$V = Ed = 24525 \times 6 \times 10^{-3} = 147 \, V$$

9. Electrons are accelerated from rest through a PD of 5000 V in an evacuated tube, then they enter a uniform magnetic field B of flux density 10^{-3} T which is at right angles to the electron beam as shown in the diagram below.

Calculate the speed of the electrons on entering the magnetic field.

$$eV = \frac{1}{2}mv^2$$

$$v = \sqrt{\frac{2eV}{m}} = \sqrt{\frac{2 \times 1.6 \times 10^{-19} \times 5000}{9.1 \times 10^{-31}}} = 41931393 \ m/s$$

Calculate the magnitude of the force experienced by the electron in the magnetic field

$$F = evB = 1.6 \times 10^{-19} \times 41931393 \times 10^{-3} = 6.7 \times 10^{-15} N$$

Calculate the radius of the path of the electron.

$$evB = \frac{mv^2}{r}$$

$$r = \frac{mv}{eB} = 0.238 \ m$$

10. The diagram below shows a heated filament which acts as an electron source in an evacuated cathode ray tube.

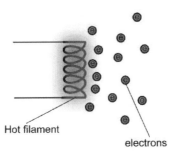

Hot filament

electrons

The specific charge of electrons is 1.8×10^{11} C/kg. Calculate the acceleration voltage required to accelerate the electrons in the beam to maximum speed of 1×10^7 m/s

$$eV = \frac{1}{2}mv^2$$

$$V = \frac{mv^2}{2e} = \frac{v^2}{2\frac{e}{m}} = 0.5 \times \frac{(1 \times 10^7)^2}{1.8 \times 10^{11}} = 277.7 \, V$$

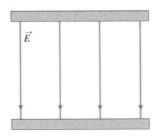

The beam of electrons from the filament passes through a vertical electric field.

State how the velocities of the electrons will be affected

From the diagram above, the top plate is positive, which results in the electrons will be deflected towards the top plate. The electrons accelerated upwards. There will be no change in the horizontal velocity of electrons.

Describe fully the direction of a suitable magnetic field that could be superimposed on the electric field so that electrons with a single speed v would pass through the combined fields without deflection.

18

The electric field will produce an electrostatic force upwards. A magnetic field with a downward force is needed. Based on the Fleming's left-hand rule, a magnetic with a field lines going into the paper will produce a downward force on a negative charge.

Derive a relation between electric field strength E and magnetic field strength B and the electron speed v for this condition of zero deflection.

$$evB = eE$$

$$v = \frac{E}{B}$$

*11.a) An electron of mass m, charge e travels with speed v in a circle of radius r in a plane perpendicular to a uniform magnetic field strength B.

i) Write down a algebraic equation relating the centripetal and electromagnetic forces acting on the electron.

$$evB = \frac{mv^2}{r}$$

$$r = \frac{mv}{eB}$$

ii) Derive an algebraic equation for the time period
using $F = m\omega^2 r = e\omega rB$

$$\omega = \frac{e}{m}B$$

$$T = 2\pi\frac{e}{m}B$$

b) If the speed of the electron changed to 2v, what effect, if any, would this change have on:

the orbital radius r,
if the velocity doubled then r will double

the orbital period T?

the time period stays the same id speed is doubled

c) Radio waves from outer space are used to obtain information about interstellar magnetic fields. These waves are produced by electrons moving in circular orbits. The radio wave frequency is the same as the electron orbital frequency.

If waves of frequency 1.2 MHz are observed, calculate:
the orbital period of the electrons;

$$T = \frac{1}{f} = \frac{1}{1.2 \times 10^6} = 8.3 \times 10^{-6}s$$

the flux density of the magnetic field.

$$2\pi f = \frac{e}{m} B$$

$$B = \frac{2\pi f m}{e} = 4.28 \times 10^{-5}T$$

12.Two parallel metal sheets of length 20 cm are separated by 2 cm in a vacuum. A narrow beam of electrons enters symmetrically between them as shown below.

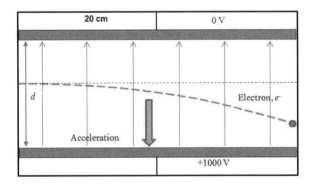

When a PD of 1000 V is applied between the plates the electron beam just misses one of the plates as it emerges.

Calculate the speed of the electrons as they enter the gap. $e/m = 1.8 \times 10^{11}$ C/kg

$$s = ut + \frac{1}{2}at^2 = \frac{1}{2}at^2$$

$$eE = ma$$

$$e\frac{V}{d} = ma$$

$$a = \frac{e}{m}\frac{V}{d} = 8.79 \times 10^{15}\ ms^{-2}$$

$$t^2 = \frac{2s}{a}$$

$$t = 1.5 \times 10^{-9}\ s$$

$$v = \frac{x}{t} = \frac{0.02}{1.5 \times 10^{-9}}\ 132598708\ m/s$$

13. A heated filament and an anode with a small hole in it are mounted in an evacuated glass tube so that a narrow beam of electrons emerges vertically upwards from the hole in the anode. A uniform magnetic field is applied so that the electrons describe a circular path in a vertical plane.

a) Derive an expression for the specific electric charge e/m of the electrons in terms of the PD between the anode and filament, V, the radius of the circular path, r, and the magnetic flux density, B.

$$r = \frac{mv}{eB}$$

$$eV = \frac{1}{2}mv^2$$

$$v = \sqrt{\frac{2eV}{m}}$$

21

$$r = \frac{m}{eB} \sqrt{\frac{2eV}{m}}$$

$$\frac{e}{m} = \frac{2V}{r^2 B^2}$$

b) What value of B would be required to give a radius of the electron path of 2r, assuming V remain constant.

Half B will result in double the radius

If B is now held constant at it's a new value, what value of V will restore the beam to its former value.

four times the voltage to decrease the r to its original value.

14. Electrons from a hot cathode emerge from a small hole in a conical shaped anode and the path subsequently followed is made visible by the gas in the tube. (e/m = 1.8×10^{11} C/kg)

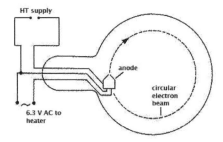

The accelerating voltage is 6300 V. Calculate the speed of the electrons as they emerge from the anode.

$$eV = \frac{1}{2}mv^2$$

$$v = \sqrt{\frac{2eV}{m}} = \sqrt{2V\frac{e}{m}}$$

22

$$v = \sqrt{2 \times 6300 \times 1.8 \times 10^{11}} = 47623523 \; m/s$$

The apparatus is situated in a uniform magnetic field. Explain why the path is circular. Calculate the radius of the circular path for flux density 0.002 T.

$$\frac{mv^2}{r} = evB$$

$$r = \frac{mv}{eB} = \frac{v}{\frac{e}{m}B} = 7.55 \; m$$

Millikan's Oil Drop Experiment

This experiment, devised by Millikan in 1909, used electric fields to deduce the charge on an electron. Fine droplets of oil were sprayed through a hole in a horizontal plate and allowed to drift down through the air between it and a lower plate. The principle of Millikan's experiment is to measure the terminal velocity of a small, charged oil drop falling under the weight of gravity. It then opposes its motion with an electric field in such a way that it remains stationary. As the drops come out of the atomiser, they are charged by friction. If no electric field is applied between A and B, then the oil drops fall downwards by the action of gravity. During this fall, their motion is opposed by the viscosity of air.

Suppose a given drop of mass, m, acquires a charge q_1. If oil drop is stationary, then if the potential is adjusted so that the electrostatic force upwards balances the gravitational force downwards then:

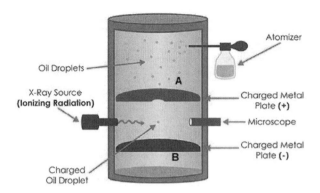

Figure 1.11 Millikan's experiment apparatus

$$mg = Eq_1 = q_1\frac{V}{d} \ --(1.9)$$

where E is the field between the plates, V is the potential difference between them and d their separation.

$$q_1 = \frac{mgd}{V} \ ---(1.10)$$

Millikan repeated the experiment many times and obtained a series of results for different droplets with different masses and charges.

He found that all the charges were multiples of one basic charge namely 1.6×10^{-19} C. He reasoned that since he found no charge of smaller value then this must be the charge on the electron. Millikan established the quantisation of electric charge.

If the oil drop is in motion, then it is known from hydrodynamics that when a spherical object of radius r falls through a fluid having the coefficient of viscosity n, then it attains a constant terminal velocity v after falling through some distance.

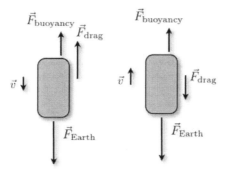

Figure 1.12 Force on oil drop

Once the drop has reached its terminal velocity, it has no acceleration and therefore

Weight = Upthrust due to air ($F_{Buoyancy}$) + Viscous drag -------- (1.11)

Weight = Volume of drop × Density of oil × g

$$Weight = \frac{4}{3}\pi r^3 \rho_o g \quad \text{------ (1.12)}$$

Where r is the radius of the drop and ρ_o is the density of oil

The Upthrust = Weight of air displaced by drop = Volume of drop × Density of air × g

$$Upthrust = \frac{4}{3}\pi r^3 \rho_a g \quad \text{------- (1.13)}$$

where ρ_a is the density of air

By Stokes' Law

$$Viscous\ drag = 6\pi r \eta v \quad \text{----- (1.14)}$$

where η is coefficient of viscosity of air.

Applying equations (1.12), (1.13) and (1.14) in (1.11)

$$\frac{4}{3}\pi r^3 \rho_o g = \frac{4}{3}\pi r^3 \rho_a g + 6\pi r\eta v \text{ ------ (1.15)}$$

When an electric field has been applied such that the drop is stationary, the forces acting on the drop are

Weight = Upthrust + Electric Force

$$\frac{4}{3}\pi r^3 \rho_o g = \frac{4}{3}\pi r^3 \rho_a g + qE \text{ ----- (1.16)}$$

Subtracting equations (1.15) from (1.16)

$$0 = qE - 6\pi r\eta v \text{ -------- (1.17)}$$

$$q = \frac{6\pi r\eta v}{E} \text{ ----------------(1.18)}$$

$$\frac{4}{3}\pi r^3(\rho_o - \rho_a)g = 6\pi r\eta v \text{ ------ (1.19)}$$

$$r = \sqrt{\frac{9\eta v}{2(\rho_o-\rho_a)g}} \text{ ----------------(1.20)}$$

$$q = \frac{6\pi\eta}{E}\sqrt{\frac{9\eta v}{2(\rho_o - \rho_a)g}} \text{ ---- (1.21)}$$

Examples

15. a) Explain what is meant by quantization of charge.

Charge could only exist as a multiple of a constant value.

b) A cloud of oil droplets is formed between two horizontal parallel metal plates.

Explain the following observation:
In the absence of an electric field between the plates, all the oil droplets fall slowly at uniform speeds.

The oil droplet falls at its terminal velocity

On applying a vertical electric field, some droplet speeds are unaltered, some are increased downwards, where some droplets move upwards.

Some of droplets are unaltered because they are uncharged. There is an increase in speed downwards because they are charged with the same charge as the plate above. Some droplets move upwards because they have an opposite charge to the plate at top.

16. Robert Millikan observed the motion of the charged oil droplets between two oppositely charged horizontal plates 5 mm apart. In such experiment, a charged droplet of mass 9.8×10^{-16} kg was balanced by the upward electric force created by PD of 300 V between the plates.

a) If the top plate was positive with respect to the bottom plate, what was the sign of the charge on the droplet?

The charge on droplets are negative.

b) Calculate
i) the electric field strength between the plates,

$$E = \frac{V}{d}$$

$$E = \frac{300}{0.005} = 60000$$

ii) the charge on the droplet

$$mg = qE$$

$$q = \frac{mg}{E} = \frac{9.8 \times 10^{-16}}{60000} = 1.6 \times 10^{-19} C$$

c) What conclusions did Millikan come to after measuring the charge on the many individual droplets?

Charge comes in integer multiple of constant value of 1.6 × 10⁻¹⁹ C

17. a) A charged oil drop falls at constant speed in the Millikan oil-drop experiment when there is no PD between the plates. Explain Why?

The droplets reached terminal velocity.

b) Such an oil drop, of mass 4×10^{-15} kg, is held stationary when an electric field is applied between the two horizontal plates. If the drop carries 6 electric charges each of value 1.6×10^{-19} C, calculate the value of the electric strength. Assume g = 9.8 N/kg

$$mg = qE$$

$$E = \frac{mg}{q} = \frac{4 \times 10^{-15} \times 9.81}{1.6 \times 10^{-19}} = 40875 \ V/m$$

18. In measurement of the electron charge by Millikan's method, a potential difference of 1.5 kV can be applied between horizontal parallel metal plates 12 mm apart. With the field switched off, a drop of oil of mass 10^{-14} kg is observed to fall with constant velocity 400 μm/s. When the field is switched on, the drop rises with constant velocity 80μm/s. How many electron charges are there on the drop? (Assume the air resistance proportional to the velocity of the drop and that air buoyancy may be neglected.

$$mg = 6\pi\eta r v$$

$$9.81 \times 10^{-14} = 6\pi\eta r \times 400 \times 10^{-6}$$

$$6\pi\eta r = \frac{9.81 \times 10^{-14}}{400 \times 10^{-6}}$$

$$9.81 \times 10^{-14} = 6\pi\eta r \times 80 \times 10^{-6} + qE$$

$$9.81 \times 10^{-14} = \frac{9.81 \times 10^{-14}}{400 \times 10^{-6}} \times 80 \times 10^{-6} + q\frac{1500}{0.012}$$

$$\frac{1500}{0.012}q = 9.81 \times 10^{-14} - \frac{9.81 \times 10^{-14}}{400 \times 10^{-6}} \times 80 \times 10^{-6}$$

$$q = 3.99\ e \approx 4e$$

19. In Millikan's experiment an oil drop of mass 1.92×10^{-14} kg is stationary in the space between the two horizontal plates which are 2.00×10^{-2} m apart, the upper plate being earthed and the lower one at a potential of -6000 V.

State, with the reason, the sign of the electric charge on the drop. Neglecting the buoyancy of the air, calculate the magnitude of the charge.

The electric charge is negative, as the top plate is positive.

$$qE = mg$$

$$q = \frac{mg}{E} = \frac{1.92 \times 10^{-14} \times 9.81}{\dfrac{6000}{0.02}} = 6.278 \times 10^{-19} C$$

With no change in the potentials of the plates, the drop suddenly moves upwards and attains a uniform velocity.
Explain why

(i) the drop moves,

The droplet has gained another charge.

(ii) the velocity becomes uniform.

The droplet reached its terminal velocity

Chapter 2

Theories of Light

In the seventeenth century two rival theories of the nature of light were proposed; the wave theory and the corpuscular theory.

Newton's particle theory of light

Newton proposed that light consists of little masses. This means that a horizontal beam of light near the earth is undergoing projectile motion and forms a parabola. The straight line we observe is due to the fact that the speed of the particles is so great.

Many known properties of light could be explained easily by a particle model. For example, it is known that when light reflects from a smooth surface, the angle of incidence is equal to the angle of reflection. This is also how an elastic, frictionless ball bounces from a smooth surface.

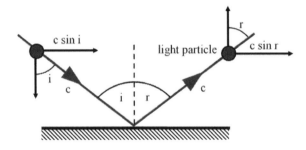

Figure 2.1 Reflection according to Newton's particle theory of light

Consider a particle of light in collision with the surface of a mirror. The collision is supposed to be perfectly elastic, and so the component of velocity perpendicular to the mirror is reversed while that parallel to the mirror remains unaltered.

Component of velocity before collision parallel to the mirror = c sin i

Component of velocity after collision parallel to the mirror = c sin r

Therefore,

c sin i = c sin r

the angle of incident, i = the angle of reflection, r

A key property for the particle theory is refraction.

Refraction

Newton imagined that matter is made of particles of some kind. When a light particle is deep within a medium, such as water or glass, it is surrounded on all sides by equal numbers of these particles. Suppose there is an attractive force between the light particles and the matter particles. Then deep within a medium, these forces cancel each other out and there is no net force on the light particle.

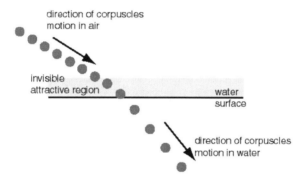

Figure 2.2 Refraction according to Newton's particle theory of light

Then, according to Newton's first law, the light particle will continue moving in a straight line since no net force acts on it. Near an interface, the situation is different. Now there are more matter particles on one side than the other, and the light particle can experience a net force. It would experience a brief attractive force towards the medium with more matter particles.

As the light particle moves into the water, it experiences a brief attractive force towards the water. This increases the vertical component of its velocity. Since it did not experience any net horizontal force, its horizontal velocity remains the same. This brief vertical force speeds the light particle

31

up, and deflects its velocity towards the surface normal, which is what is observed.

He explained total internal reflection by saying that the perpendicular component of velocity was too small to overcome the molecular attraction. This has the effect of increasing the velocity of the light in the material.

Let the velocity of light in air be c_a and the velocity of light in the material is c_m.

The velocity parallel to the material is unaltered and therefore:

$c_a \sin i = c_m \sin r$

Therefore:

$$\frac{c_m}{c_a} = \frac{\sin i}{\sin r} = {}_a n_m \text{ ------(2.1)}$$

This ratio is the refractive index, but because n > 1 the velocity of light in the material must be greater than that in air.

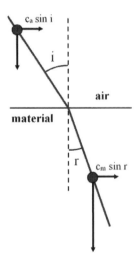

Figure 2.3 Velocity distribution light particle

Dispersion

Newton's explanation for the fact that a prism separates a beam of white light into the colours of the rainbow was simple. We have seen that red light refracts least, and violet light most. Newton stated that the mass of the light particle varied with colour. Red light particles have more mass than violet. As a result, they will be deflected less upon crossing an interface between materials. He assumed all light particles experience the same force on crossing an interface. What differs among them is their inertia. Red light particles with more inertia will be deflected less by the same force than violet light particles.

Huygens' wave theory of light

In 1678, Huygens proposed a model where each point on a wave front may be regarded as a source of waves expanding from that point. The expanding waves may be demonstrated in a ripple tank by sending plane waves toward a barrier with a small opening. If waves approaching a beach strike a barrier with a small opening, the waves may be seen to expand from the opening. He believed that light was a longitudinal wave, and that this wave was propagated through a material called the 'aether' or 'ether'

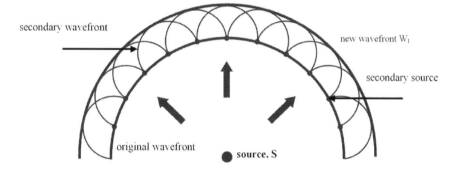

Figure 2.4 Propagation of wave

There are, however, at least two problems with this idea and these led Newton and others to reject it:

(a) the secondary waves are propagated in the forward direction only, and
(b) they are assumed to destroy each other except where they form the new wave front.

Huygens' theory also failed to explain the rectilinear propagation of light (in straight lines).

Reflection

Consider a parallel beam of monochromatic light incident on a plane surface, as shown in the figure 2.5. The wave fronts will be plane both before and after reflection, since a plane surface does not alter the shape of waves falling on it.

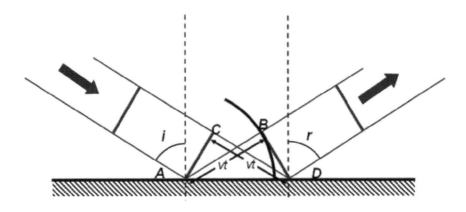

Figure 2.5 Reflection according wave theory

From the diagram above,

AB = CD

Angle ACB = angle ADB = 90°

AD is common

Therefore ΔCAD and ΔBDA are similar and so angle CAB = angle BAC. Therefore, i = r and the law of reflection is proved.

Refraction

Consider a plane monochromatic wave hitting the surface of a transparent material of refractive index n.

The velocity of light in the material is c_m and that in air c_a.

34

CB = AB sin i

AD = AB sin r

The same argument applies about the new envelope as in the case of reflection:

Time to travel CB = CB/c_a = AB sin i/c_a, time to travel AD AD/c_m = AB sin i/c_m

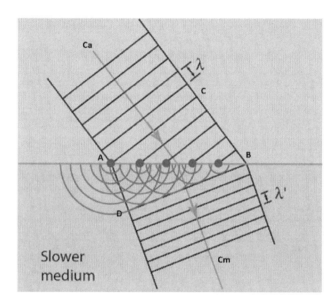

Figure 2.6 Refraction according wave theory

But these are equal and therefore:

$$\frac{c_a}{c_m} = \frac{sini}{sinr} = {_m}n_a$$

This is Snell's law, and it was verified later by Foucault and others. Notice that since the refractive index of a transparent material is greater than 1, Huygens' theory requires that the velocity of light in air should be greater than that in the material.

Young's double slit experiment

The first serious challenge to the particle theory of light was made by the English scientist Thomas Young in 1803.Young knew that sound was a wave phenomenon, and, hence, that if two sound waves of equal intensity, but 180° out of phase, reach the ear then they cancel one another out, and no sound is heard. This phenomenon is called interference.

Young reasoned that if light were a wave phenomenon, as he suspected, then a similar interference effect should occur for light. This line of reasoning lead Young to perform an experiment which is nowadays referred to as Young's double-slit experiment.

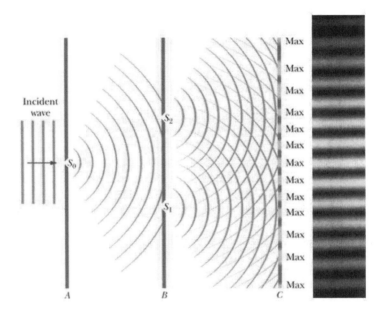

Figure 2.6 Diffraction and interference of Monochromatic light

A monochromatic light source is incident on the first screen which contains a slit S_0. The emerging light then arrives at the second screen which has two parallel slits S_1 and S_2. which serve as the sources of coherent light. The light waves emerging from the two slits then interfere and form an interference pattern on the viewing screen. The bright bands or fringes correspond to interference maxima, and the dark band interference minima.

The formula for a maximum is:

36

nλ = d sin θ where d is the distance between the centres of the two slits and n is the order number.

The intensity of the interference pattern produced by two sources is simply varied by the diffraction effects.

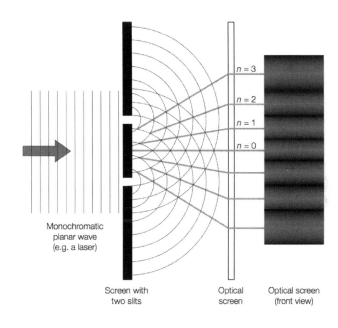

Figure 2.7 Double slit Interference of light

If white light is used, a white centre fringe is observed. But all the other fringes have coloured edges, the blue edge being nearer the centre. Eventually the fringes overlap, and a uniform white light is produced.
The separation of the two slits should be of the same order of magnitude as the wavelength of the radiation used.

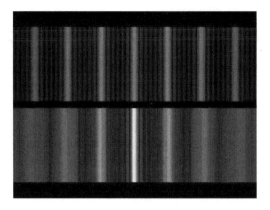

Figure 2.8 Double slit Interference of monochromatic and white light

Electromagnetic radiation

James Clerk Maxwell's theory had predicted that electromagnetic disturbances should propagate through space at the speed of light and should exhibit the wave-like characteristics of light propagation.

The electric and magnetic field components of plane electromagnetic waves are perpendicular to each other and also perpendicular to the direction of wave propagation.

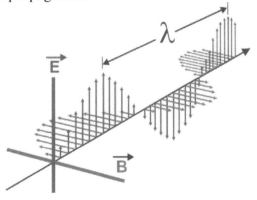

Figure 2.9 Electromagnetic wave

The relative magnitudes of E and B in empty space are related by $c = \frac{E}{B}$

We can write the velocity of electromagnetic waves in free space is given by the following equation:

$$c = \frac{1}{\sqrt{\varepsilon_o \mu_o}} \quad ---(2.2)$$

where ε_o is the permittivity of free space and μ_o is the permeability of free space.

All e-m radiations have the same properties:

> it is propagated by varying electric and magnetic fields oscillating at right angles to each other;
> it travels with a constant velocity of 299 792 458 ms^{-1} in a vacuum;
> it is unaffected by electric and magnetic fields;
> it travels in straight lines in a vacuum;
> it may be polarised;
> it can show interference and diffraction.

Heinrich Hertz's Wireless Experiment

According to theory, if electromagnetic waves were spreading from the oscillator sparks, they would induce a current in the loop that would send sparks across the gap. This occurred when Hertz turned on the oscillator, producing the first transmission and reception of electromagnetic waves. Hertz also noted that electrical conductors reflect the waves and that they can be focused by concave reflectors. He found that non-conductors allow most of the waves to pass through. Another of his discoveries was the photoelectric effect.

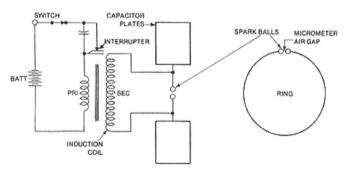

Figure 2.10 Hertz's experiment diagram

An induction coil is connected to two spherical electrodes. There is a narrow gap between them. The coil provides short voltage surges to the spheres, making one positive, the other negative. A spark is generated between the spheres when the voltage between them reaches the breakdown voltage for air. As the air in the gap is ionized, it conducts more readily and the discharge between the spheres becomes oscillatory. From an electrical circuit viewpoint, this is equivalent to an LC circuit, where the inductance is that of the loop and the capacitance is due to the spherical electrodes.

Electromagnetic waves are radiated at this frequency as a result of the oscillation (and hence acceleration) of free charges in the loop. Hertz was able to detect these waves using a single loop of wire with its own spark gap (the receiver). This loop, placed several meters from the transmitter, has its own effective inductance, capacitance, and natural frequency of oscillation. Sparks were induced across the gap of the receiving electrodes when the frequency of the receiver was adjusted to match that of the transmitter. Thus, Hertz demonstrated that the oscillating current induced in the receiver was produced by electromagnetic waves radiated by the transmitter. Hertz's experiment is analogous to the mechanical Phenomenon in which a tuning fork picks up the vibrations from another, identical oscillating tuning fork.

Fizeau speed of light

A French physicist, Fizeau, shone a light between the teeth of a rapidly rotating toothed wheel. A mirror more than five miles away reflected the beam back through the same gap between the teeth of the wheel. There were over a hundred teeth in the wheel. The wheel rotated at hundreds of times a second; therefore, a fraction of a second was easy to measure. By varying the speed of the wheel, it was possible to determine at what speed the wheel was spinning too fast for the light to pass through the gap between the teeth, to the remote mirror, and then back through the same gap. He knew how far the light travelled and the time it took. By dividing that distance by the time, he got the speed of light. Fizeau measured the speed of light to be 313,300 km/s.

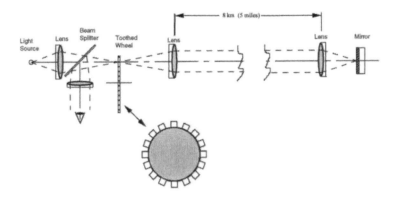

Figure 2.11 Calculating speed light

Emission of Radiation

Quantum theory was first introduced in Physics by Max Plank in1900 while trying to explain the observed energy distribution of the electromagnetic radiation emitted by a blackbody. It is well known that when a body is heated, it emits electromagnetic radiation. When a piece of iron is heated to a few hundred degrees centigrade, it emits e-m radiation which is predominantly in the region in the infra red radiation. When the temperature is raised further to 1000 °C, it begins to glow with reddish colour which shows that the radiation emitted by it has a shorter wavelength. As it gets hotter and hotter, so the radiation emitted has a shorter and shorter wavelength. There is a spread of wavelengths emitted and it is the majority of the radiation that is emitted at shorter wavelengths, as the temperature rises.

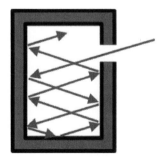

Figure 2.12 Blackbody

41

Apart of emitting e.m. radiation, a heated body also absorbs part of the radiation falling on it. A black body is a body which absorbs all the radiation incident on it. A black body radiator is a theoretical object that is totally absorbent to all thermal energy that falls on it, thus it does not reflect any light so appears black. As it absorbs energy, it heats up and re-radiates the energy as electromagnetic radiation.

Black-body radiation does not depend on the nature of the emitting surface, but it does depend upon its temperature.

The shift in the peak of the intensity distribution curves as temperature is changed is found to obey Wien's displacement law.

$$\lambda_m T = constant \quad --- (2.3)$$

The total power E radiated per unit area of a black body of a blackbody is found to depends on its absolute temperature.

$$E = \sigma T^4 \quad --- (2.4)$$

The above equation called Stefan-Boltzmann law

$\sigma = 5.67 \times 10^{-8} \ W/m^2$

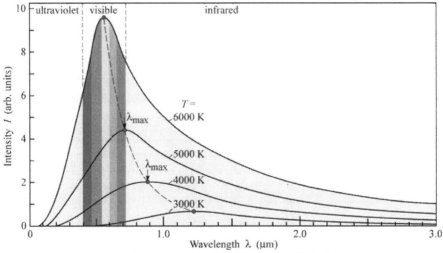

Figure 2.12 Spectral distribution of blackbody

42

Rayleigh-Jeans Law

Using classical Physics, they derive an equation to radiation distribution spectrum from black body. Electromagnetic spectrum predicted by their formula agrees with experimental results at low frequencies (large wavelengths) but strongly disagrees at high frequencies (short wavelengths). This inconsistency between observations and the predictions of classical physics is commonly known as the ultraviolet.

From the equation below, As $\lambda \rightarrow 0, E_\lambda \rightarrow \infty$

$$E_\lambda = \int \frac{8\pi kT}{\lambda^4} \, d\lambda$$

The Rayleigh-Jeans Law was an important step in our understanding of the equilibrium radiation from a hot object, even though it turned out not to be an accurate description of nature. The careful work in developing the Rayleigh-Jeans law laid the foundation for the quantum understanding expressed in the Planck radiation formula.

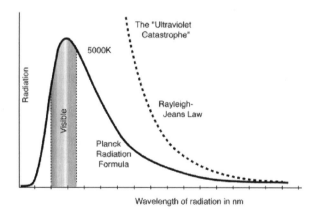

Figure 2.13 Ultraviolet Catastrophe

In 1900, the problem was solved in a revolutionary way by Max Planck. He has to invent a new Physics to solve the problem. He proposed that radiation was emitted not in a continuous stream of energy, but in bundles of energy that he called quanta. He related the energy of a quantum to its frequency by the formula:

43

$$Eenergy\ (E) = hf \quad ----(2.5)$$

Where h is a constant known as Planck's constant and its value is 6.626×10^{-34} Js and f is frequency of the emitted light.

since $f = \frac{c}{\lambda}$ we could write the energy formula

$$Eenergy\ (E) = h\frac{c}{\lambda}$$

Planck reasoned that this formula covered all electromagnetic radiation.

$$E_\lambda = \frac{8\pi hc}{\lambda}\ \frac{1}{e^{\frac{hc}{\lambda kT}}-1} \quad ----(2.6)$$

Where E_λ is the power per unit volume per wavelength, k is Boltzmann constant, h is Planck's constant, c is speed of light

Photoelectric effect

Photoelectric emission is the emission of electrons from the surface of a metal when it is exposed to electromagnetic radiation of sufficient high frequency.

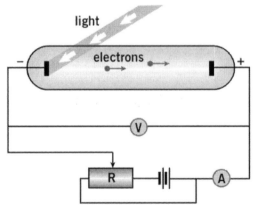

Figure 2.14 Photoelectric experiment circuit diagram

Experiments show that:

Increasing the intensity of the light increases the number of electrons emitted per second.

For light beneath a certain threshold frequency, f_o, no electrons are emitted, even in very intense light.

Above f_o, the maximum KE of the electrons increases with frequency, but is not affected by intensity. Even very dim light gives some electrons with high KE.

The wave theory cannot explain the threshold frequency, or how low-amplitude waves can cause high-KE electrons.

The wave theory

The wave theory of electromagnetic radiation predicts that emission of photoelectrons should happen at all frequencies. Electrons in metal would absorb energy continuously from radiation of any frequency and be emitted when they had absorbed enough energy. This process would take longer at lower frequencies but should still happen. In addition, there should be no maximum kinetic energy of the emitted electrons

The wave theory could not explain experimental results. Metals like zinc emit photoelectrons when illuminated by X-rays and ultraviolet radiation. No photoelectrons are emitted from zinc when illuminated by blue light or by any other light from the visible range, regardless of the light intensity.

Quantum theory

According to the quantum theory of electromagnetic radiation, the Photon energy is directly proportional to frequency of light.

$$E = hf$$

Where h is Planck constant = 6.63×10^{-34} Js, f is frequency.

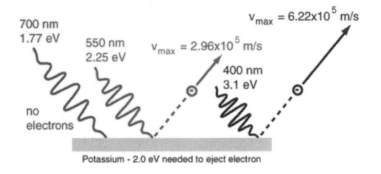

Figure 2.15 Emission of photoelectrons

Einstein suggested that when a photon causes photoelectric emission from a metal surface, some of the photon energy is used to overcome the work function (i.e. it provides the energy needed to liberate a surface electron) while the remainder appears as kinetic energy of the ejected electron. This is very succinctly expressed in Einstein's photoelectric equation:

$$hf = \phi + E_k \text{------(2.7)}$$

The above equation is a conservation of energy equation

hf is the energy of incident photon

ϕ is the Work function

E_k is the maximum kinetic energy of freed electron, where $= \frac{1}{2}mv_{max}^2$, v_{max}^2 is the maximum velocity of the electron. Most photoelectrons will have energies less than the maximum value. This is because electrons emitted from atomic layers beneath the metal surface lose energy in collisions with atoms on their way out of the metal.

The work function of a material is the work necessary to remove an electron from the surface of the material.

Threshold frequency f_0 is the minimum frequency required for the photoelectron emission.

46

Equation 2.7 can be expressed in terms of wavelength, λ of the incident photon using the formula $f = \frac{c}{\lambda}$

$$h\frac{c}{\lambda} = \phi + E_k \quad \text{-----(2.8)}$$

$$h\frac{c}{\lambda} = \phi + \frac{1}{2}mv_{max}^2 \quad \text{--------(2.9)}$$

Equation 2.7 shows that the maximum kinetic energy of a photoelectron depends only on the frequency of the photon. A more intense beam (i.e. brighter light) simply contains more photons per second, and will produce more photoelectrons, but will not affect their maximum kinetic energy. Photoelectrons can only escape if the maximum kinetic energy is greater than zero:

$$hf - \phi > 0$$

or $f > \frac{\phi}{h}$

So, the minimum frequency (f_o) (also called the threshold frequency) required to cause photoemission from a metal of work function ϕ is given by:

$$f_o = \frac{\phi}{h} \quad \text{-----(2.10)}$$

Stopping potential

If the surface of the metal is positively charged, the photoelectrons will have to lose more of their kinetic energy in order to overcome the increased attraction force between the electrons and the positive charge of the metal. Increasing the positive potential will reduce the number of electrons escaping per second as a smaller proportion will have the necessary energy to overcome the increased attraction.

$$E_k = hf - \phi - eV \quad \text{-----(2.11)}$$

where e is the electric charge and V is the applied potential.

If the potential is increased further, a value will be reached at which photoemission is just prevented. This value is known as the stopping potential (V_s)

Since the maximum kinetic energy has been i to zero:

$$eV_s = hf - \phi \quad ---(2.12)$$

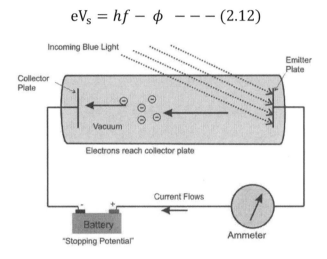

Figure 2.16 Stopping potential circuit diagram

If we plot the stopping potential as function of frequency, we get the graph below.

The graph figure 2.17 tells that the higher the frequency of the light falling on the photoelectric plate, the higher the stopping potential needed to stop the photoelectrons.

$$V_s = \frac{h}{e}f - \frac{\phi}{e} \quad ----(2.13)$$

The gradient of the above graph is $\frac{h}{e}$, the intercept with x axis is f_0 and the intercept with y axis is $\frac{\phi}{e}$

To find the Planck's constant h = gradient × charge of electron

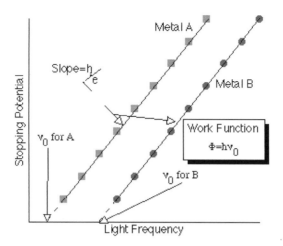

Figure 2.17 Stopping potential as function of frequency

Increasing the light intensity does not affect the energy of the photoelectron and therefore does not affect the stopping potential.

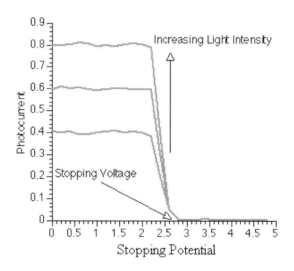

Figure 2.18 Photocurrent as function of stopping potential

Summary

The number of electrons emitted per second from any metal is directly proportional to the intensity of the radiation falling on it. Intensity is the power per unit surface area.

49

The photoelectrons are emitted from a given metal with a range of kinetic energies, from zero up to a maximum. The maximum energy increases with the frequency of the radiation and is independent of the intensity of the radiation. Shining a brighter light of the same colour produces more photoelectrons per second but does not increase their kinetic energies.

For each metal, there is a minimum frequency required to produce emission. This is called the threshold frequency (f_o). (Similarly, there is a corresponding threshold wavelength, above which no emission can occur.) Radiation below this frequency cannot produce emission, no matter how intense the radiation. So, even a bright industrial laser (visible light) cannot cause photoemission from zinc, whereas a weak ultra-violet source can.

The higher frequency light, the higher energy per photon which results in higher energy needed to stop the photoelectrons or higher stopping potential.

Wave-Particle Duality

The phenomena of reflection, refraction, interference and diffraction can all be explained using the idea of light as a wave motion. Furthermore, the fact that light can be polarised indicates that the waves are transverse. But when it comes to explaining the photoelectric effect, we need to think of the electromagnetic radiation as having particle properties.

So, which of our two models is a correct description of light?

Is it a wave motion or a particle motion?

The answer of course is that both ideas are merely different models which help us to explain how electromagnetic radiation behaves in different circumstances; neither is a perfect or full description.

Based on the idea that light and all other electromagnetic radiation is both particle and wave, Louis de Broglie suggested that the same kind of dual nature must also be applicable to matter. He proposed that any particle of matter of momentum (p) has an associated wavelength (λ) given by

$$\lambda = \frac{h}{p} \text{ -----------------(2.14)}$$

Where h is the Planck constant and $p = mv$

$$\lambda = \frac{h}{mv} \text{ --------------------(2.15)}$$

m is the mass, v is the velocity of the object.

$$E = \frac{1}{2}mv^2 = eV \text{ --------(2.16)}$$

from (3) we could write $v = \sqrt{\frac{2eV}{m}}$

$$p = m\sqrt{\frac{2eV}{m}} = \sqrt{2eVm}$$

$$\lambda = \frac{h}{\sqrt{2eVm}} \text{ -----------------(2.17)}$$

For accelerating potentials of about 100 V, the associated wavelength of an electron is about 10^{-10} m. This is the same order of magnitude as X-ray wavelengths. Since diffraction of X-rays (and other electromagnetic radiation) is explained by considering their wave properties, it follows that diffraction of beams of electrons would confirm that they too had wave properties.

This was confirmed in 1926 by Davison and Germer, who demonstrated diffraction of a beam of electrons by a single crystal of nickel. The distance between the planes of atoms in the crystal is of the same order of magnitude as the de Broglie wavelength of the election beam, thus producing significant diffraction.

Figure 2.19a Electron diffraction

Diffraction effects have since been observed with beams of protons, neutrons and even α-particles. However, as equation 2.15 indicates, the associated wavelength decreases as mass increases, making diffraction effects more difficult to observe with more massive particles. Diffraction of a beam of electrons directed at a crystal or a thin metal foil is shown figure 2.19b.

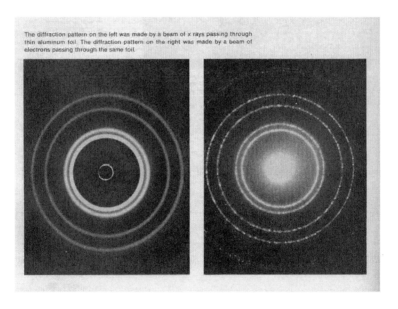

Figure 2.19b Electron diffraction compared with x-ray diffraction

The diffraction pattern produced is a set of concentric circles. The angular deflection of the diffracted electrons can be calculated, to provide information about the spacing between the atoms in the metal foil, in much the same way as X-ray diffraction. This wave-like behaviour of electrons is used in electron microscopes, in which beams of electrons are used instead of light to provide magnified images. At high accelerating voltages, the wavelengths of the electrons are much shorter than light wavelengths, so much finer detail can be resolved. The field ion microscope uses beams of helium ions, with an even smaller wavelength, leading to the ability to resolve individual molecules.

The de Broglie wavelength, $\lambda = \dfrac{h}{mv}$ is a matter wave not electromagnetic wave. The speed of the de Broglie wave is equal to the speed of the object it is associated with.

For matter wave $\lambda = \dfrac{v}{f}$ not $\lambda = \dfrac{c}{f}$

The electron microscope

The electron microscope is based on the discovery by Thomson, Davisson and Germer that electrons have wave properties. If an electron is accelerated through a p.d. of 500 000 V, then the wavelength associated with it is

$$\lambda = \frac{h}{\sqrt{2eVm}}$$

$$= \frac{6.63 \times 10^{-34}}{\sqrt{2 \times 1.6 \times 10^{-19} \times 500000 \times 9.1 \times 10^{-31}}} = 1.73 \times 10^{-12}$$

This means that if it can be used in a microscope the resolving power, which depends on wavelength, would be very large.

Electrons are also affected by magnetic fields, and magnetic focusing had been used for some time in the cathode ray tube. By combining several such magnetic lenses, a succession of magnifications may be obtained.

The condenser lens produces a parallel beam of electrons which strike the object. Some electrons are absorbed by the object, some are transmitted, and some are scattered sideways. These scattered electrons cannot pass through the small slit placed in front of the object. In order to reduce the number of scattered electrons the object must be very thin.

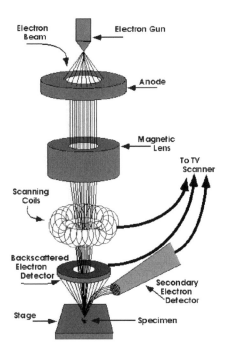

Figure 2.20 Electron Microscope

The transmitted electrons pass through one or two magnifying lenses and the final image is formed on a screen or on a photographic plate. Electron diffraction in Transmission Electron Microscope (TEM) is subject to several important limitations.

Firstly, the sample to be studied must be electron transparent, meaning the sample thickness must be of the order of 100 nm or less.

Secondly, other problems exist at these very high magnifications: the objects that we are trying to view are little larger, by a factor of 1000 or so, than the electrons in the beam and so the electron beam distorts the object. In addition, the very high-energy electrons leak across the viewing screen, so blurring the image further.

Thirdly, the electrons are emitted from the cathode with a range of energies and therefore do not all have the same velocity and wavelength. Since the trajectory of the electron depend on its speed, electrons from the same point on the object can end up at different points on the image-an effect analogous to chromatic aberration.

Finally, the focal length of a magnetic lens depends on the current in its coil. Small fluctuations in the current will affect the focusing of the image.

The Scanning Tunnelling Microscope

The scanning tunnelling microscope was invented in 1981 by Gerd Binnig and Heinrich Rohrer. The STM is a non-optical electron based microscope which employs the quantum mechanical effect of tunnelling. It works by scanning a very sharp metal tip over a conducting surface within a range of several angstroms of it. When the tip is brought to such a close distance from the sample and a bias voltage is applied between the tip and the sample, a tunnelling current flow through the vacuum gap that separates the two conductors, even though they are not in electrical contact.

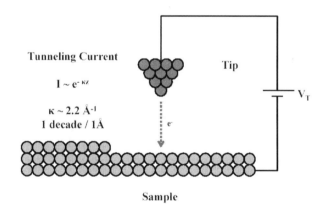

Figure 2.21 Tunnelling microscope circuit diagram

The tip is mounted on a piezo tube which undergoes a mechanical deformation because of the applied electric field. Therefore, the position of the tip is locally changed along the lateral and vertical direction. The set point value for the current is determined by the user. During normal operation, the tunnelling current is held constant using a feedback circuit.

Once a stable tunnel junction is achieved, the tip is raster scanned over the surface and its position is varied via the distortions of the piezoelectric actuator, so that the current remains constant. When this operating mode is used, images are created recording the vertical position required to keep the current constant. These images contain information about the geometry and electronic structure of the surface, revealing the real-space structure of the surface under investigation. The vertical resolution in scanning tunnelling arises from the extremely high sensitivity of the tunnelling current with respect to the tip-sample distance.

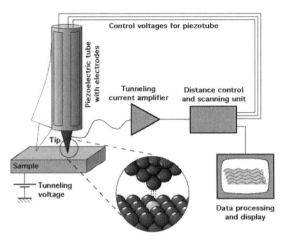

Figure 2.22 Tunnelling microscope

Examples

20. At the end of the seventeenth century Newton's corpuscular theory of light was much more widely accepted than Huygens' wave theory. Explain why.

Newton's formidable reputation.

The Wave theory of light could not explain why an opaque object in the path of a beam of light casts a sharp shadow.

Wave theory cannot explain how light can travel through vacuum without a medium.

21. Thomas Young demonstrated interference of light using a double-slits arrangement and a candle flame which is a light source that emits a continuous spectrum of light. The same phenomenon can be demonstrated using monochromatic light from a laser. Give two reasons why interference fringes produced by a candle flame are much more difficult to observe than fringes produced by a laser beam.

The fringe width is proportional to the wavelength. In the case of a white light, the red light fringes of the first order overlap the blue light fringes which make measurement very difficult. The light from the candle flickers which makes the fringes shift or change location, which makes the fringe width difficult.

22. Calculate the energy of (a) a photon of frequency 7.0 x 10 ^{14} Hz, (b) a photon of wavelength 3.0 × 10^{-7} m. (h= 6.6 × 10^{-34} J s, c = 3.0 × 10^8 m/s.)

$$E = hf = h\frac{c}{\lambda} = 6.63 \times 10^{-34} \times \frac{3 \times 10^8}{3.0 \times 10^{-7}} = 6.63 \times 10^{-19} J$$

23. Calcium has a work function of 2.7 eV. (a) What is the work function of calcium expressed in joules? (b) What is the threshold frequency for calcium? (c) What is the maximum wavelength that will cause emission from calcium?

$\phi = 2.7 \times 1.6 \times 10^{-19} = 4.32 \times 10^{-19}$ J

$\phi = hf_o$

$$f_o = \frac{\phi}{h} = \frac{4.32 \times 10^{-19}}{6.63 \times 10^{-34}} = 6.5 \times 10^{14} Hz$$

$$\lambda_o = \frac{c}{f_o} = \frac{3 \times 10^8}{6.5 \times 10^{14}} = 4.6 \times 10^{-7} m$$

24.Gold has a work function of 4.9 eV (a) Calculate the maximum kinetic energy, of the electrons emitted when gold is illuminated with ultraviolet radiation of frequency 1.7 × 10^{15} Hz. (b) is this energy expressed in eV? (c) What is the stopping potential for these electrons?

$$hf = \emptyset + E_{max}$$

$$E_{max} = 6.63 \times 10^{-34} \times 1.7 \times 10^{15} - 4.9 \times 1.6 \times 10^{-19}$$

$$E_{max} = 3.43 \times 10^{-19}$$

$$E_{max} = 2.14 \ eV$$

$$E_{max} = eVs$$

Vs = 2.14 volts

25. Calculate the stopping potential for a platinum surface irradiated with ultraviolet light of wavelength 1.2×10^{-7} m. The work function of platinum is 6.3 eV

$$hf = \emptyset + E_{max}$$

$$hf = \emptyset + eV_s$$

$$h\frac{c}{\lambda} = \emptyset + eV_s$$

$$eV_s = h\frac{c}{\lambda} - \emptyset$$

$$eV_s = 6.63 \times 10^{-34}\frac{3 \times 10^8}{1.6 \times 10} - 6.3 \times 1.6 \times 10^{-19}$$

Vs = 4.06 V

26. Draw a graph showing the distribution of energy in the spectrum of a black body. Explain what quantity is plotted against the wavelength. By considering how this energy distribution varies with temperature explain the colour changes which occur when a piece of iron is heated from cold to near its melting point.

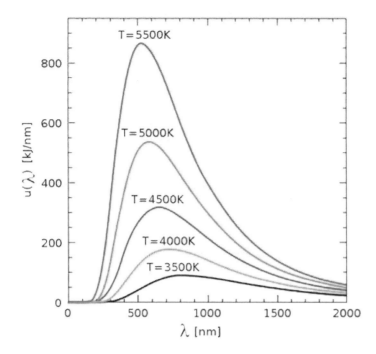

At low temperatures, all energy emitted is in the infrared range. Increasing the temperature will result in more of the radiation emitted in the visible range but mainly the red part of the spectrum. Increasing the temperature more will result in more of visible light and more of the light in green and blue part of the spectrum. Increasing the temperature more will result in visible light emitted and more in blue part of spectrum.

27. The silica cylinder of a radiant wall heater is 0.6 m long and has a radius of 5 mm. If it is rated at 1.5 kW estimate its temperature when operating. State two assumptions you have made in making your estimate. (Stefan's constant, $\sigma = 6 \times 10^8$ W/m²K⁴.)

$$A = 0.6 \times \pi \times (5 \times 10^{-3})^2 = 4.71 \times 10^{-5} m^2$$

$$E = \sigma A T^4$$

$$T = \sqrt[4]{\frac{E}{\sigma A}} = \sqrt[4]{\frac{1500}{6 \times 10^8 \times 4.71 \times 10^{-5}}} = 479.9\ K$$

59

28. The diagram shows how E$_\lambda$, the energy radiated per unit area per second per unit wavelength interval, varies with wavelength λ for radiation from the Sun's surface.

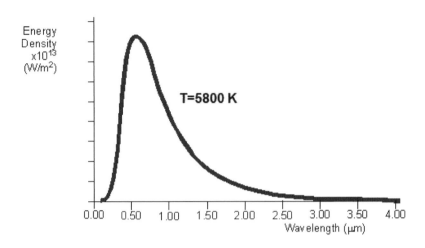

a) Calculate the wavelengths at which the corresponding curves peak for: radiation in the Sun's core where the temperature is approximately 15×10^6 K, and

$$\lambda_{max}T = constant$$

$$\lambda_{max1}T_1 = \lambda_{max2}T_2$$

$$\lambda_{max2} = \frac{5800 \times 0.6 \times 10^{-6}}{15 \times 10^6} = 2.32 \times 10^{-10}m$$

x-ray

b) radiation in interstellar space which corresponds to a temperature of approximately 2.7K.

Name the part of the electromagnetic spectrum to which the calculated wavelength belongs in each case.

$$\lambda_{max}T = constant$$

$$\lambda_{max1}T_1 = \lambda_{max2}T_2$$

$$\lambda_{max2} = \frac{5800 \times 0.6 \times 10^{-6}}{2.7} = 0.00128 \ m$$

Infrared near the microwave range

29. The solar radiation falling normally on the surface of the Earth has an intensity 1.40 kWm^{-2}. If this radiation fell normally on one side of a thin, freely suspended blackened metal plate and the temperature of the surroundings was 300 K, calculate the equilibrium temperature of the plate. Assume that all heat interchange is by radiation.
(Stefan's constant 5.67 x 10^{-8} Wm^{-2} K^{-4})

$$E = \sigma(T^4 - T_o^4)$$

$$T^4 = \frac{E}{\sigma} - T_o^4$$

$$T^4 = \frac{1400}{5.67 \times 10^{-8}} - 300^4$$

T= 425.56 K

30. The total power output of the Sun is 3.79×10^{26} W. Calculate
a) the temperature of the Sun's surface,

b) the wavelength at which the Sun radiates the maximum energy.
(Diameter of Sun 1.39×10^9 m, σ= 5.67×10^{-8} Wm^{-2} K^{-4})

$$\lambda_{max}T = 2.9 \times 10^{-3}$$

a)

$$E = \frac{P}{A} = \frac{3.79 \times 10^{26}}{3.14 \times \frac{1.39 \times 10^{26}}{2}} = 1.37 \times 10^{17} \frac{W}{m^2}$$

$$E = \sigma T^4$$

$$T = \sqrt[4]{\frac{E}{\sigma}} = \sqrt[4]{\frac{1.37 \times 10^{17}}{5.67 \times 10^{-8}}} = 1.32 \times 10^{6} K$$

b)

$$\lambda_{max} T = 2.9 \times 10^{-3}$$

$$\lambda_{max} = \frac{2.9 \times 10^{-3}}{1.32 \times 10^{6}} = 2.19 \times 10^{-9} m$$

31. Light of frequency 6.0×10^{14} Hz incident on a metal surface ejects photoelectrons having a kinetic energy 2.0×10^{-19} J.

Calculate the energy needed to remove an electron from the metal. Very briefly indicate how you would determine experimentally the kinetic energy of the photoelectrons.

$$hf = \emptyset + E_{max}$$

$$\emptyset = hf - E_{max}$$

$$= 6.63 \times 10^{-34} \times 6 \times 10^{14} - 2 \times 10^{-19} = 1.98 \times 10^{-19}$$

To determine the kinetic energy experimentally

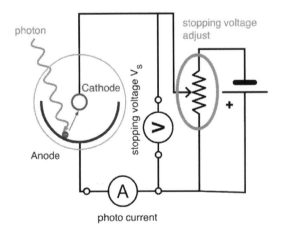

Firstly, connect an anode to a positive terminal of power supply as in the diagram above. Secondly, radiate the anode with monochromatic light with a frequency large enough for electrons to be emitted. Increase the voltage until all electrons have been repelled by the cathode and attracted by the anode, current = 0. The voltage of the voltmeter is the stopping potential. Thirdly, Calculate the kinetic energy using

$$E_{max} = eV_s$$

32. Light of wavelength 0.50 μm incident on a metal surface ejects electrons with kinetic energies up to a maximum value of 2.0×10^{-19} J. What is the energy required to remove an electron from the metal? If a beam of light causes no electrons to be emitted, however great its intensity, what condition must be satisfied by its wavelength? (The Planck constant 6.6×10^{-34} J s, the speed of light 3.0×10^8 m/s)

$$h\frac{c}{\lambda} = \phi + E_{max}$$

$$\phi = h\frac{c}{\lambda} - E_{max}$$

$$\phi = 6.63 \times 10^{-34} \frac{3 \times 10^8}{0.5 \times 10^{-6}} - 2 \times 10^{-19}$$

$\phi = 1.98 \times 10^{-19}$ J

33. The maximum kinetic energy of photoelectrons ejected from a tungsten surface by monochromatic light of wavelength 248 nm was found to be 8.6×10^{-20} J. Find the work function of tungsten.

(The Planck constant, $h = 6.6 \times 10^{-34}$ J s; speed of light, $c = 3.0 \times 10^8$ m/s , electronic charge, $e = -1.6 \times 10^{-19}$ C)

$$h\frac{c}{\lambda} = \phi + E_{max}$$

$$\phi = h\frac{c}{\lambda} - E_{max}$$

$\phi = 7.16 \times 10^{-19}$ J

34. Einstein's equation for the photoelectric emission of electrons from a metal surface under radiation of frequency f can be written as

$$hf = \frac{1}{2}mv^2 + \emptyset$$

where m is the mass of an electron, v the greatest speed with which an electron can emerge and $\emptyset$ is a quantity called the work function of the metal.

Explain briefly the physical process with which this equation is concerned.

$$hf = \frac{1}{2}mv^2 + \emptyset$$

The above equation is conservation of energy equation.

Describe briefly an experiment by which you could determine the values of h/e and

Using $hf = eVs + \emptyset$

$$Vs = \frac{h}{e}f - \frac{\emptyset}{e}$$

It is clear from the above equation that the stopping potential is proportional to the frequency. Measure the stopping potential for each frequency. Plot f against Vs as in the graph below. The gradient is $\frac{h}{e}$ and the intercept with y axis is $\frac{\emptyset}{e}$.

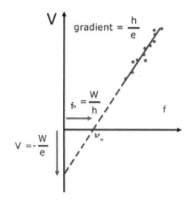

For sodium the value of ϕ is 3.12 × 10⁻¹⁹ J, and the wavelength of sodium yellow light is 590 nm.

Explain why electrons are emitted when a sodium surface is irradiated with sodium yellow light and calculate the greatest speed of the emitted electrons.

Sodium yellow light supply more energy to the electron on the surface of the metal greater than the work function.

$$h\frac{c}{\lambda} = \frac{1}{2}mv^2 + \emptyset$$

$$v = \sqrt{\frac{2(hc - \emptyset\lambda)}{m\lambda}}$$

$$v = \sqrt{\frac{2(6.63 \times 10^{-34} \times 3 \times 10^8 - 3.12 \times 10^{-19} \times 590 \times 10^{-9})}{590 \times 10^{-9} \times 9.1 \times 10^{-31}}}$$

v = 234959 m/s

Estimate the 'stopping potential' for these electrons, assuming that no contact potential differences are involved.

$$eVs = \frac{1}{2}mv^2$$

$$Vs = \frac{1}{2}\frac{m}{e}v^2 = 0.5 \times \frac{9.1 \times 10^{-31}}{1.6 \times 10^{-19}} \times (234959)^2 = 0.15\,V$$

35. (a) When electromagnetic radiation falls on a metal surface, electrons may be emitted. This is the photoelectric effect.

i) State Einstein's photoelectric equation, explaining the meaning of each term.

$$hf = \emptyset + \text{Emax}$$

hf is the photon energy

$\emptyset$ is work function: is the minimum amount of energy needed to remove an electron from the surface of the metal.

Emax is the maximum kinetic energy of the emitted photoelectrons

ii) Explain why, for a particular metal, electrons are emitted only when the frequency of the incident radiation is greater than a certain value.

The energy of the photon is directly proportional to the frequency of the photon. If the frequency of the photon is greater than the threshold frequency, an electron emitted.

iii) Explain why the maximum speed of the emitted electrons is independent of the intensity of the incident radiation.

The intensity of light does not increase the energy of photons, only increasing the number of photons. Each electron is emitted when one photon is absorbed by the electron. Increasing the number of photons does not increase the energy of each photon.

b) A source emits monochromatic light of frequency 5.5×10^{14} Hz at a rate of 0.10 W. Of the photons given out, 0.15% fall on the cathode of a photocell which gives a current of 6.0 μA in an external circuit. You may assume this current consists of all the photoelectrons emitted.

Calculate:

i) the energy of a photon,

$$E = hf = 6.63 \times 10^{-34} \times 5.5 \times 10^{14} = 3.64 \times 10^{-19} J$$

ii) the number of photons leaving the source per second,

$$n_p = \frac{0.1}{3.64 \times 10^{-19}} = 2.74 \times 10^{17}$$

iii) the percentage of the photons falling on the cathode which produce photoelectrons.

$$n_e = \frac{6 \times 10^{-6}}{1.6 \times 10^{-19}} = 3.75 \times 10^{13}$$

Number of photons falling on the cathode

$$n_p = \frac{0.15}{100} \times 2.74 \times 10^{17} = 4.11 \times 10^{14}$$

$$\% \, photons = \frac{3.75 \times 10^{13}}{4.11 \times 10^{14}} \times 100 = 9.12\%$$

c) Calculate the wavelength associated with electrons which have been accelerated from rest through 3000 V.

$$\lambda = \frac{h}{mv}$$

$$eV = \frac{1}{2}mv^2$$

$$v = \sqrt{\frac{2eV}{m}}$$

$$\lambda = \frac{h}{m\sqrt{\frac{2eV}{m}}}$$

$$\lambda = \frac{h}{\sqrt{2meV}} = \frac{6.63 \times 10^{-34}}{\sqrt{2 \times 9.1 \times 10^{-31} \times 1.6 \times 10^{-19} \times 3000}}$$

$$\lambda = 2.24 \times 10^{-11} m$$

36. Light of photon energy 3.5 eV is incident on a plane photocathode of work function 2.5 V. Parallel and close to the cathode is a plane collecting electrode. The cathode and collector are mounted in an evacuated tube.

a) Find the maximum kinetic energy E_{max} of photoelectrons emitted from the cathode.

$$hf = \emptyset + E_{max}$$

$$E_{max} = hf - \emptyset$$

$$E_{max} = 3.5 - 2.5 = 1 \, eV = 1.6 \times 10^{-19} J$$

b) Find the minimum value of the potential difference which should be applied between collector and cathode in order to prevent electrons of energy E_{max} from reaching the collector for electrons emitted

$$E_{max} = eVs$$

Vs = 1 volt

37. Calculate the de Broglie wavelength of an electron moving at 3.0 × 10⁷.

$$\lambda = \frac{h}{mv} = \frac{6.63 \times 10^{-34}}{9.1 \times 10^{-31} \times 3 \times 10^7} = 2.43 \times 10^{-11} m$$

38. Calculate the de Broglie wavelength of an electron which has been accelerated from rest through a PD of 40 V.

$$\lambda = \frac{h}{mv}$$

$$eV = \frac{1}{2}mv^2$$

$$\lambda = \frac{h}{\sqrt{2meV}} = \frac{6.63 \times 10^{-34}}{\sqrt{2 \times 9.1 \times 10^{-31} \times 1.6 \times 10^{-19} \times 40}}$$

$$= 1.94 \times 10^{-10} m$$

39. What is the ratio of the de Broglie wavelength of an electron to that of a proton (a) if they both have the same energy (Mass of electron 9.1×10^{-31} kg, mass of proton 1.67×10^{-27} kg.)

$$\lambda_e = \frac{h}{P_e}$$

Where Pe is the momentum of an electron

$$E = \frac{1}{2}mv^2 = \frac{p^2}{2m}$$

If $E_e = E_p$

$$\frac{P_e^2}{2m_e} = \frac{P_p^2}{2m_p}$$

$$\frac{2m_e}{2m_p} = \frac{P_p^2}{P_e^2}$$

$$\frac{\lambda_e}{\lambda_p} = \frac{P_p^2}{P_e^2} = \sqrt{\frac{m_p}{m_e}} = 42.83$$

(b) if they both have the same speed?

$$\lambda_e = \frac{h}{m_e v_e}$$

$$\lambda_p = \frac{h}{m_p v_p}$$

$$\frac{\lambda_e}{\lambda_p} = \frac{m_p}{m_e} = 1835$$

Chapter 3

The Theory of Relativity

The Michelson Morley experiment

In 1865, Maxwell predicted the existence of electromagnetic waves. Starting from the fundamental equations of electricity and magnetism, he was able to show that an oscillating charge should send out waves. These waves consist of oscillating electric and magnetic fields, which are usually at right angles to each other and to the direction of propagation. Their existence was confirmed by Hertz in 1888.

At the time when electromagnetic waves were discovered, all known types of wave (e.g. sound waves, water waves) travelled in some kind of material medium. It was therefore natural to assume that electromagnetic waves also had their medium, provisionally named the aether, and attempts were made to detect it. But the aether proved very elusive, although it must be present everywhere where light can be transmitted, even in a vacuum or in interstellar space. All attempts to measure its density or elastic modulus, or indeed any other property, failed to obtain positive results.

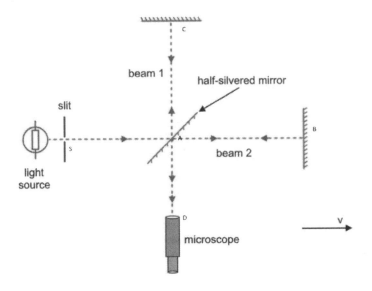

Figure 3.1 Michelson Morley experiment

Suppose that one beam of light is split into two which are sent along different paths and then recombined. Interference fringes will be formed, and any difference in the times taken to traverse the two paths will show up as a shift in the position of the dark and bright fringes.

A time difference Δt is equivalent to a path difference of $c\Delta t$, and will thus shift the pattern by $c\Delta t / \lambda$ (width of one fringe), where λ is the wavelength of the light.

In 1881, Michelson set up the experiment shown figure 3.1. Light from the sources is split into two beams by the half-silvered mirror A. After reflection from mirrors B and C, the beams are recombined and produce fringes which are viewed through the eyepiece D. (B and C are not quite perpendicular, producing parallel fringes, as with a wedge.)

The arms AB and AC are of equal length L.

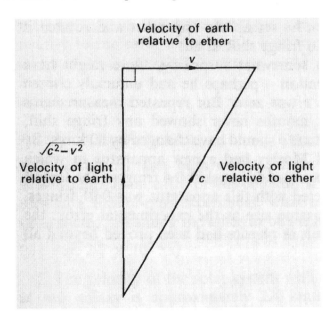

Figure 3.2 Effect of aether velocity on velocity of light

Suppose the earth is moving through the aether with velocity v in the direction AB. The round- trip time for light following path ABA is

$$t_1 = \frac{L}{c - v} + \frac{L}{c + v} = \frac{2Lc}{c^2 - v^2}$$

$$t_1 = \frac{2Lc}{c^2 - v^2} = \frac{2L}{c}\left(1 - \frac{v^2}{c^2}\right)^{-1}$$

Using $(1 + x)^n \approx 1 + nx + \cdots$ for $x \ll 1$

$$t_1 = \frac{2L}{c}\left(1 + \frac{v^2}{c^2}\right)^{-1} \approx \frac{2L}{c}\left(1 + \frac{v^2}{c^2} + \cdots\right) - - - (3.1)$$

From S to B the relative speed is c+v and from B to S the relative speed is c-v.

The light travelling from A to C must have a component of velocity v along AB, relative to the aether, or it will fail to strike the mirror at C.

Since the total velocity of the light relative to the aether is c, subtracting this component leaves a velocity of $\sqrt{c^2 - v^2}$ along AC.

The same is true for the return journey, so the total time for path ACA is $\frac{2L}{\sqrt{c^2-v^2}}$

$$t_2 = \frac{2L}{\sqrt{c^2 - v^2}} = \frac{2L}{c}\left(1 - \frac{v^2}{c^2}\right)^{-\frac{1}{2}}$$

Since $v \ll c$

$$t_2 = \frac{2L}{c}\left(1 - \frac{v^2}{c^2}\right)^{-\frac{1}{2}} \approx \frac{2L}{c}\left(1 + \frac{1}{2}\frac{v^2}{c^2} + \cdots\right)$$

The time difference between the two beams is

72

$$\Delta t = t_1 - t_2 \approx \frac{2L}{c}\left\{(1+\frac{v^2}{c^2}) - (1+\frac{1}{2}\frac{v^2}{c^2})\right\}$$

$$\Delta t \approx \frac{L}{c} \cdot \frac{v^2}{c^2}$$

frequency shift

$$\Delta f = \frac{c\Delta t}{\lambda} = \frac{L}{\lambda} \cdot \frac{v^2}{c^2} \; - - - (3.2)$$

The easiest way of measuring the fringe shift is to rotate the whole apparatus through 90°. Since this interchanges arms AB and AC and reverses the sign of the fringe shift, an overall shift of $2\Delta f$ should be observed. Michelson's first apparatus had arms 1.2 m long; with $\lambda = 6 \times 10^{-7}$ m and $v = 10^{-4}c$, he expected a shift of 0.04 fringes, or twice the least shift he could detect. However, when he set up the apparatus and rotated it carefully, there was no fringe shift at all.

Although this was somewhat surprising, there might have been a simple explanation. Perhaps he had unluckily chosen a time of year when v was zero. But repeated measurements over a period of six months never showed any fringe shift, although during that time v should have changed by 60 km/s. By 1887, Michelson and Morley had a new apparatus in which L was 11 m and the expected fringe shift 0.4 fringes. The largest fringe shift ever detected with this apparatus was 0.01 fringes, which was about the same size as the experimental error: the most famous null result in physics had been proved beyond all reasonable doubt.

Explanations of the null result
Many attempts were made to explain the non-existence of the fringe shift. One was to suppose that the aether near the earth is dragged along with it: If this were true, any experiment carried out wholly on the earth would always show it to be apparently at rest in the aether. But astronomical evidence was available to prove that aether drag did not exist.

Another explanation, proposed by Fitzgerald and shown by Lorentz to follow from the electromagnetic theory of matter, was for all lengths parallel to the direction of the earth's motion through the aether to be contracted by a $\sqrt{1 - \frac{v^2}{c^2}}$. This would explain the Michelson-Morley result for apparatus with arms of equal length. But it would predict a fringe shift on rotating an apparatus with unequal arms. Kennedy and Thorndike (1932) used an unequal arms apparatus but failed to detect any shift.

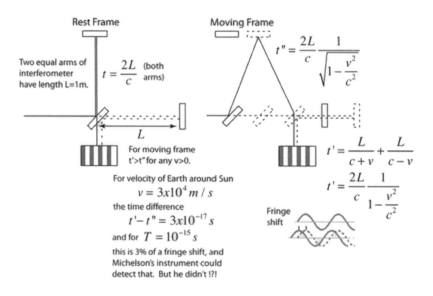

Figure 3.3 Null result

Einstein's solution was simple: the velocity of light with respect to the earth is always c, whether the earth moves through the aether or not. This obviously explains the Michelson-Morley result as the round- trip time is always 2L/c for any path but makes nonsense of the addition of velocities. If the velocity of light is c and the velocity of the earth is v, both relative to the aether and in the same direction, then the velocity of light relative to the earth must be c-v and cannot be c. This was so basic it just couldn't be wrong, until Einstein proved that it was.

Coordinate system

A coordinate system provides a way of identifying a particular point in space. This is usually done by taking three mutually perpendicular lines as axis and specifying coordinates *x, y, z* as the perpendicular distances from the point to the corresponding axis. (An alternative name for 'coordinate system' is 'frame of reference'.)

The point where the axis meet is the origin *O* of the coordinate system and the coordinates of a point are usually written *(x, y, z)*. The coordinate system as a whole is denoted by S.

Relativity is concerned with how the same events appear when viewed in different coordinate systems.

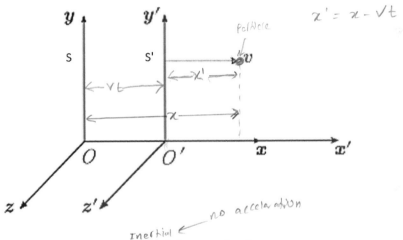

Figure 3.4 Initial frame of reference

Let us compare events as seen in *S* and in a second coordinate system S', with origin at *O'* and coordinates x', y' and z'.

In general, the behaviour of the same object may appear to be quite different in *S* and in *S'*.

But in a coordinate system fixed to the sun, the bench and indeed the whole laboratory is not stationary but rotates round the origin once a year, not to mention the complicated motion due to the earth's turning on its axis once every 24 hours.

75

Everything is much simpler if S and S' have constant relative velocity. Coordinate systems related in this way are called *inertial frame of reference*. Let us assume that *O* and *O'* coincide at time *t* = 0 and that *O'* then moves along *Ox* with velocity *v,* as shown in Fig. above. Then the two sets of coordinates *(x, y, z)* and *(x', y', z')* representing the same point in S and in S' are related by equations

$$x' = x - vt, \qquad y' = y, \qquad z' = z$$

These are usually called the Galilean transformation.

Inertial Frames of reference

Inertial Frames of reference are frames where Newton's First Law is true. That is, if an object experiences no net force, the object either remains at rest or continues in motion with constant speed in a straight line.

If the airplane is not accelerating, it's an inertial reference system.

In 1905, Albert Einstein published the theory of special relativity, which explains how to interpret motion between different inertial frames of reference, that is, places that are moving at constant speeds relative to each other.

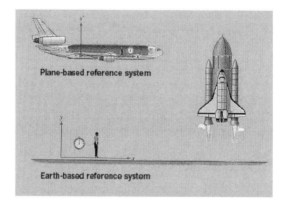

Figure 3.5 Relative time

76

Measurements made in the train are relative to the train and the train is therefore one frame of reference, while measurements made at the side of the track are relative to the ground, the other frame of reference. For example, if you swing a ball round your head in the train on a piece of string, you see it moving in a circle while someone watching from the side of the track will see it move in a much more complicated orbit.

Both observers say that the ball's motion is exactly as expected from the acceleration caused by the pull of the earth.

Both observers see the ball behaving as Newton's laws and gravitational force predict it should.

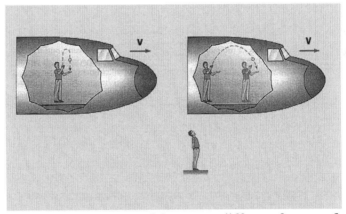

Figure 3.6 Motion of ball as observed from two different frames of reference

Assumptions in relativity

Einstein made two vital assumptions or postulates when he proposed the theory of relativity and these are:

- Physical laws are obeyed in all frames of reference,
- The velocity of light in free space is constant in all inertial frames of reference.

If we assume these, then we must abandon some of our other more traditional ideas, such as the constancy of mass, length and time. This means that if one object is moving relative to a frame of reference, then the mass and length of the body measured from the frame of reference will be different from those measured with instruments travelling with the body. Even more unusual, time measured by a clock travelling with the body will differ from that measured by a clock at rest in the frame of reference.

Length appears to get smaller, mass increases and time appears to pass more slowly in a moving frame of reference when viewed from a stationary frame. Any such differences are very small, however, unless the relative velocities are very large, that is, approaching that of light.

Time Dilation

Imagine a person in a train with a torch. They shine the beam of the torch across the carriage and time how long it takes to return to them. Very simply it is just the distance the light travels (twice the width of the carriage (L) divided by the speed of light (c). Someone on the embankment by the train will also agree with the measurement of the time that the light beam takes to get back to the person with the torch after reflecting from the mirror.

They will both say that the time (t) is 2L/c.

Now consider what happens as the train moves at a constant speed along the track.

The person in the train still considers that the light has gone from the torch, straight across the carriage and returned to them. It has still travelled a distance of 2L and if the speed of light is c the time (t) it has taken is 2L/c.

However, to the person on the embankment this is not the case. They will observe the light beam moving a distance given by the equation:

Distance travelled by light according to an observer on the bank = $2 [L^2 +s^2]^{1/2}$ because the train has moved along a distance s while the light beam crosses the train and returns to the observer.

Now in classical physics, we would now say that since the light beam has moved further in the same time it must be moving faster, in other words we have to "add" the speed of the train to the speed of the light. But the theory of relativity does not allow us to do this. It says that the speed of light is constant. So, we must alter something else. The "something else" is the time, we have to assume that the light has had longer to travel the greater

78

distance, in other words more time has passed for the observer on the bank than for the observer in the carriage. This is called time dilation.

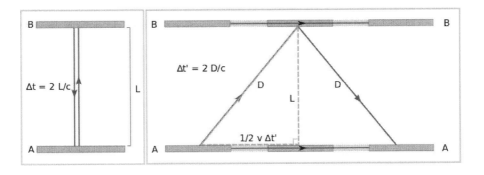

Figure 3.7 Time dilation

We will call the time for the "stationary" observer on the embankment t.

If the train moves at a speed v we have:

$$Time\ taken\ t = \frac{2s}{v} = \frac{2[L^2 + s^2]^{\frac{1}{2}}}{c}$$

$$t^2 = \frac{4[L^2 + s^2]}{c^2}$$

But

$$t = \frac{2s}{v} \quad and\ s = \frac{tv}{2}$$

And

$$D = \frac{ct_0}{2}$$

$$t^2 = \frac{4L^2}{c^2} + \frac{4s^2}{c^2} = t_0^2 + t^2 \frac{v^2}{c^2}$$

79

$$t\left(1 - \frac{v^2}{c^2}\right) = t_0$$

Time passed as noted by the stationary observer

$$t = \frac{t_0}{\sqrt{1 - \frac{v^2}{c^2}}} \quad ---(3.3)$$

The observer on the bank thinks that a longer time interval has passed than the person in the train.

The extended half-life of fast-moving muons

The slowing down of time or time dilation has been noticed in atomic clocks that have been carried in satellites. But a natural phenomenon that supports time dilation is the decay of fast-moving muons as they travel downwards through the atmosphere.

High energy cosmic ray protons entering the upper atmosphere interact with the nuclei of oxygen and nitrogen atoms to give a group of pions and these then decay into muons that then move off at a speed of up to 0.994 c. These muons are formed at a height of between ten and fifteen thousand metres above the ground.

The half-life of a muon is 2.2 microseconds and so even moving at 0.994 c they would only expect to travel about 660 m before half of them decayed. Muons formed at 12000 m would take 40 µs or about 20 half lives to reach the ground. This would mean that only $(1/2)^{20}$ of the original number would be detected. The fact that the proportion is much higher than this, means that the muons are living longer.

At 0.994c, the formula for time dilation gives the half-life for the muons to be 20 µs. This means that at 0.994c the proportion reaching the ground should be 0.25. This means that the number of muons per second detected at the ground is much greater than expected.

80

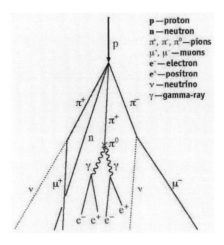

Figure 3.8 Muons Creation

The twin paradox

Suppose one of a pair of identical twins takes a quick return trip by spaceship to a nearby star, while the other stays behind on earth. The earth twin expects the astronaut twin's clocks to run slow throughout his journey, because of time dilation. Since time dilation affects all possible kinds of clock, including biological processes such as pulse or heartbeats, he therefore concludes that the astronaut twin ages more slowly and will be the younger of the two when they meet again. What does the astronaut twin think? Since he sees the earth twin move away and then approach again, our first impulse is to conclude that the experiences of the two twins are quite symmetrical. But in that case the astronaut twin will expect the earth twin to be the younger when they meet.

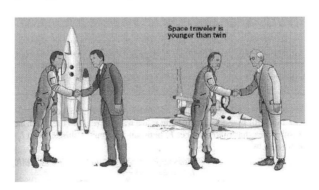

Figure 3.9 Twin paradox

81

There cannot be two correct answers. The twins must be able to agree unambiguously on which of them is the younger when they meet. Fortunately, if we look carefully at the situation, we find that there is no paradox after all. The experiences of the two twins are not symmetrical: the astronaut twin feels an acceleration when he turns around to come back to earth, while the earth twin observes nothing of the kind.

Length Contraction

As predicted by special relativity, lengths observed from the stationary reference frame look shorter than ones observed from within a reference frame moving relative to it.

The time difference Δt between the observer in the train receiving the light beams from the two lamps is insignificant at low speeds. However, it becomes larger as the speed of the train approaches that of light.

$$\Delta t_o = \frac{L}{v} \quad ---(3.4)$$

$$\Delta t = \frac{L_o}{v}$$

$$t = \frac{t_0}{\sqrt{1 - \frac{v^2}{c^2}}}$$

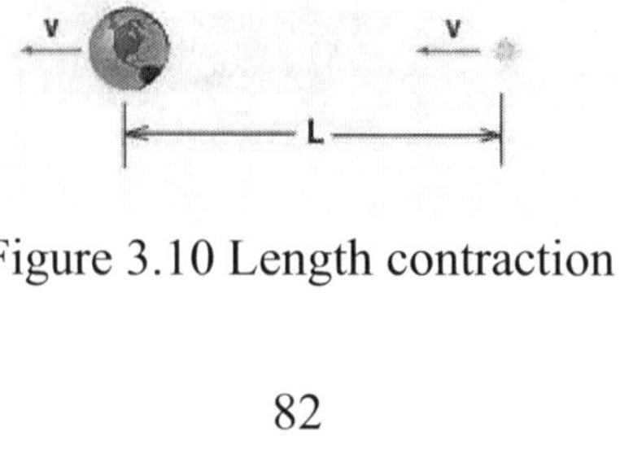

Figure 3.10 Length contraction

$$\frac{L_o}{v} = \frac{\frac{L}{v}}{\sqrt{1 - \frac{v^2}{c^2}}}$$

$$L_o = \frac{L}{\sqrt{1 - \frac{v^2}{c^2}}}$$

$$L = L_o \sqrt{1 - \frac{v^2}{c^2}} \quad ---(3.5)$$

From the above equation, we can see that, lengths parallel to the direction of motion appear to be shorter in moving coordinate systems. Lengths perpendicular to the direction of motion do not change.

Mass and Energy

Our starting point will be a "thought experiment" which was invented by Einstein himself in 1906. The purpose of it is to suggest that energy must have associated with it a certain inertial mass equivalent.

We suppose that an amount E of radiant energy (a burst of photons) is emitted from one end of a box of mass M and length L that is isolated from its surroundings and is initially stationary figure 3.11.

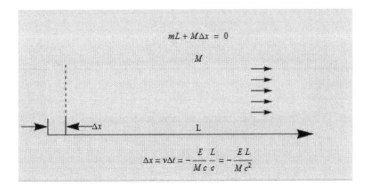

Figure 3.11 Light in a box

83

The radiation carries momentum E/c. Since the total momentum of the system remains equal to zero, the box must acquire a momentum equal E/c. Hence the box recoils with a speed v, given by $v = \dfrac{E}{Mc}$

After travelling freely for a time Δt.

$$\Delta t = \frac{L}{c} ----- (3.6) ,$$

Provided $v \ll c$.

The radiation hits the other end of the box and conveys an impulse, equal and opposite to the one it gave initially, which brings the box to rest again. Thus, the result of this process is to move the box through a distance Δx:

$$\Delta x = v\Delta t = -\frac{EL}{Mc^2} ----(3.7)$$

But this being an isolated system, we are reluctant to believe that the centre of mass of the box plus its contents has moved. We therefore postulate that the radiation has carried with it the equivalent of a mass m, such that

$$mL + M\Delta x = 0 ----(3.8)$$

Applying (3.5) and (3.6) in (3.7)

$$mL + M \times -\frac{EL}{Mc^2} = 0$$

$$mL - \frac{EL}{c^2} = 0$$

$$E = mc^2 ----(3.9)$$

From Newtonian mechanics

$$m = \frac{p}{v} ----(3.10)$$

Where p is the momentum and v is the velocity.

84

Applying (3.10) in (3.9)

$$E = \frac{c^2 p}{v} \ --- (3.11)$$

The increase in kinetic energy corresponds to the work done by external force F

$$dE = Fdx = \frac{dp}{dt} dx = \frac{dx}{dt} dp$$

$$dE = vdp \ --- (3.12)$$

$$EdE = \frac{c^2 p}{v} vdp$$

$$EdE = c^2 pdp$$

Integrating

$$E^2 = c^2 p^2 + E_0^2 \ ----- (3.13)$$

From (3.11)

$$cp = \frac{Ev}{c} \ ---- (3.14)$$

Applying (3.12) in (3.13)

$$E^2 = \left(\frac{Ev}{c}\right)^2 + E_0^2$$

$$E^2 = E^2 \frac{v^2}{c^2} + E_0^2$$

$$E^2 - E^2 \frac{v^2}{c^2} = E_0^2$$

85

$$E^2\left(1 - \frac{v^2}{c^2}\right) = E_0^2$$

$$E^2 = \frac{E_0^2}{\left(1 - \frac{v^2}{c^2}\right)}$$

$$E = \frac{E_0}{\sqrt{1 - \frac{v^2}{c^2}}} \qquad -----\ (3.15)$$

Applying (3.9) in (3.15)

$$m = \frac{m_0}{\sqrt{1 - \frac{v^2}{c^2}}} \qquad -----\ (3.16)$$

m_o is the real mass and m is the relative mass

The relativistic kinetic energy = Total energy – Rest energy

$$K = \frac{m_0 c^2}{\sqrt{1 - \frac{v^2}{c^2}}} - m_0 c^2$$

$$K = m_0 c^2 \frac{1}{\sqrt{1 - \frac{v^2}{c^2}}} - m_0 c^2$$

$$K = m_0 c^2 \left(1 - \frac{v^2}{c^2}\right)^{-\frac{1}{2}} - m_0 c^2$$

Using Taylor's Series to simplify the above equation

$$(1 + z)^n = 1 + nz + \frac{n(n-1)}{2!} z^2 + \frac{n(n-1)(n-2)}{3!} z^3 \ ....$$

86

$$(1 - \frac{v^2}{c^2})^{-\frac{1}{2}} = 1 + \frac{1}{2}\frac{v^2}{c^2} + \frac{-\frac{1}{2}(-\frac{1}{2}-1)v^4}{2!}\frac{v^4}{c^4} + \cdots$$

$$(1 - \frac{v^2}{c^2})^{-\frac{1}{2}} = 1 + \frac{1}{2}\frac{v^2}{c^2} + \frac{3}{8}\frac{v^4}{c^4} + \cdots$$

$$K = m_0c^2(1 + \frac{1}{2}\frac{v^2}{c^2} + \frac{3}{8}\frac{v^4}{c^4} + \cdots) - m_0c^2$$

$$K = m_0c^2\left(\frac{1}{2}\frac{v^2}{c^2} + \frac{3}{8}\frac{v^4}{c^4} + \cdots\right)$$

For small value of v compare to c

$$K = m_0c^2\left(\frac{1}{2}\frac{v^2}{c^2}\right) = \frac{1}{2}m_0v^2$$

Using the formula for the relativistic mass of a particle, you can see that there is kind of cosmic speed limit for matter.

Since:

$$m = \frac{m_0}{\sqrt{1 - \frac{v^2}{c^2}}}$$

at speeds close to that of light, the mass of a particle becomes very high and at v = c, the limit of further increase in speed is reached. The mass of the particle is converted into energy.

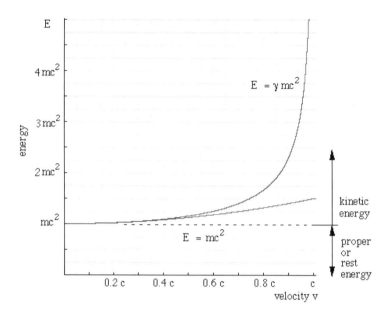

Figure 3.12 Impossibility of reaching speed of light

Examples

40. A high-intensity signal light on Earth flashes on for 1.4×10^{-5} s, as measured on Earth, as a spaceship passes overhead moving at 2.7×10^8 m. For how long is the light on from the point of view of an observer on the spaceship?

$$t = \frac{t_o}{\sqrt{1 - \dfrac{v^2}{c^2}}}$$

$$t = \frac{1.4 \times 10^{-5}}{\sqrt{1 - \dfrac{(2.7 \times 10^8)^2}{(3 \times 10^8)^2}}} = 3.21 \times 10^{-5} s$$

41. A spaceship passes the Earth at a speed of 0.8c and flashes a signal lamp for 2.0 μs. What is the duration of the signal as measured on Earth?

88

$$t = \frac{t_o}{\sqrt{1 - \dfrac{v^2}{c^2}}}$$

$$t = \frac{2 \times 10^{-6}}{\sqrt{1 - 0.8^2}} = 3.33 \times 10^{-6} \, s$$

42. The average lifetime of muons at rest in a laboratory is 2.2×10^{-6} s as measured in the laboratory. The average lifetime of muons moving at high speed in the same laboratory is found to be 6.4×10^{-6} s. At what fraction of c are these muons moving.

$$t = \frac{t_o}{\sqrt{1 - \dfrac{v^2}{c^2}}}$$

$$\frac{v^2}{c^2} = 1 - \frac{t_o^2}{t^2}$$

$$v = c\sqrt{1 - \frac{t_o^2}{t^2}}$$

$$v = c\sqrt{1 - \frac{(2.2 \times 10^{-6})^2}{(6.4 \times 10^{-6})^2}}$$

$$v = 0.989 \, c$$

43. A spaceship passing the Earth at 1.8×10^8 m/s emits a pulse of light that an observer on Earth measures as lasting for 6.4×10^{-5} s. is the duration of the pulse as measured on the spaceship?

$$t = \frac{t_o}{\sqrt{1 - \dfrac{v^2}{c^2}}}$$

$$t_o = t \sqrt{1 - \frac{v^2}{c^2}} = 6.4 \times 10^{-3} \sqrt{1 - \frac{1.8^2}{3^2}}$$

$$t_o = 5.12 \times 10^{-3} s$$

44. A muon which has a lifetime of 2.20×10^{-6} s travels through the atmosphere with a speed of 0.990c relative to the Earth.

(a) What is its lifetime as measured by an observer on the Earth?
(b) How far does the Earth observer regard the muon as travelling in this time?
(c) How far would this appear to be to someone travelling with the muon?

a)
$$t = \frac{t_o}{\sqrt{1 - \frac{v^2}{c^2}}}$$

$$t = \frac{2.2 \times 10^{-6}}{\sqrt{1 - 0.99^2}} = 1.5 \times 10^{-5} s$$

b) s = vt = 0.99c × 1.56×10⁻⁵ = 4631.0 m

c) s_o = v_ot = 0.99c × 2.2×10⁻⁶= 653.4 m

45. Observers on Earth track an alien spacecraft moving at 0.90c for 3.0 years. How far, in light years, does the craft travel in this time from point view of (a) the Earth observers, (b) the beings in the spacecraft? c) What time would have elapsed on the spacecraft?

a) s = 0.9c × 3 = 2.7 light years
b)
$$t = \frac{t_o}{\sqrt{1 - \frac{v^2}{c^2}}}$$

$$t_o = t\sqrt{1 - \frac{v^2}{c^2}} = 3\sqrt{1 - 0.9^2} = 1.3 \ years$$

$s = 0.9c \times 1.3 = 1.17$ light years

c) t = 1.3 years

46. An observer measures the length of a metre rule to be 80 cm. At what speed is rule moving relative to the observer?

$$l = l_o\sqrt{1 - \frac{v^2}{c^2}}$$

$$v = c\sqrt{1 - \frac{l^2}{l_o^2}}$$

$$v = c\sqrt{1 - 0.8^2} = 0.6c$$

47. A spaceship of length 80 m passes Earth at a speed of 0.98c. What is the length of the spaceship as measured by the observer on the Earth?

$$l = l_o\sqrt{1 - \frac{v^2}{c^2}}$$

$$l = 80 \times \sqrt{1 - 0.98^2} = 15.91 \ m$$

48. Calculate the energy released when a π^o meson decays to produce electromagnetic radiation. (Rest mass of $\pi^o = 2.4 \times 10^{-28}$ kg)

$$E = mc^2$$

$$E = 2.4 \times 10^{-28} \times (3 \times 10^8)^2 = 2.16 \times 10^{11} J$$

49. A star is 8 light-years away from the Earth. A rocket leaves Earth and travels to the star in 6 years as measured by a clock in the rocket.

a) In terms of the speed of light, c, what is the speed of the rocket relative to the Earth?

$$t = \frac{t_o}{\sqrt{1 - \frac{v^2}{c^2}}}$$

$$v = \frac{l}{t} = \frac{8c}{6 \sqrt{1 - \frac{v^2}{c^2}}}$$

$$v = \frac{8c}{6} \sqrt{1 - \frac{v^2}{c^2}}$$

$$v^2 = (\frac{8c}{6})^2 (1 - \frac{v^2}{c^2})$$

$$v = \frac{\frac{8}{6}c}{\sqrt{1 - (\frac{8}{6})^2}} = 0.8c$$

b) How long does the journey take as measured by a clock on the Earth?

$$t = \frac{6}{\sqrt{1 - 0.8^2}} = 10 \ years$$

50. The mean lifetime of muons at rest is 2.2 μs. An observer notes that they travel on average of 2000m before decaying. In terms of the speed of light, c, what is the speed of the muons relative to the observer?

$$v = \frac{do}{to} = \frac{d\sqrt{1 - \frac{v^2}{c^2}}}{to}$$

square and rearrange

$$v = \frac{909090909}{3.19} = 0.95c$$

51. A metal cube has a density of 9000 kg/m³ when at rest in the laboratory. If the cube is caused to move perpendicular to two of its faces at a speed of 2.4×10^8 m/s relative to the observer in the laboratory, what is it density as measured by the observer.

$$l = l_o\sqrt{1 - \frac{v^2}{c^2}}$$

$$Volume = l^3$$

$$Relative\ volume = l^3\sqrt{1 - \frac{v^2}{c^2}} = V_o\sqrt{1 - \frac{v^2}{c^2}}$$

$$m = \frac{m_o}{\sqrt{1 - \frac{v^2}{c^2}}}$$

$$\rho_o = \frac{M_o}{V_o}$$

$$\rho = \frac{M}{V}$$

$$\rho = \frac{M_o}{V_o\sqrt{1 - \frac{v^2}{c^2}}} = \frac{\rho_o}{\sqrt{1 - \frac{v^2}{c^2}}}$$

$$= \frac{9000}{\sqrt{1 - \frac{4^2}{5^2}}} = 15000 \; kg/m^3$$

Revision Questions

Discovery of electron and Wave particle duality

Q1.
In the figure below, a beam of monoenergetic electrons is produced by thermionic emission from a wire filament in an evacuated tube. The beam is directed at a thin metal sample at normal incidence and it emerges from the sample in certain directions only, including its initial direction.

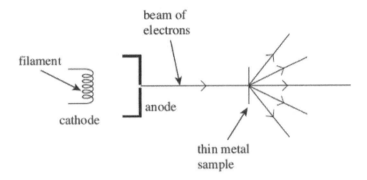

(a) (i) Name the physical process occurring at the thin metal sample in the figure above which shows the electrons behaving as waves.

(ii) Explain why the electrons need to be monoenergetic in order for them to emerge in certain directions only.

(b) A transmission electron microscope (TEM) operating at an anode potential of 25kV is used to observe an image of a thin sample.

(i) Calculate the momentum of the electrons emerging from the anode, stating an appropriate unit.

(ii) Describe and explain how the resolution of the image would change if the anode potential were increased.

Q2.

A potential difference was applied between two electrodes in a glass tube containing air, as shown in the diagram below. The pressure of the air in the tube was gradually reduced until a glow of light was observed between the electrodes.

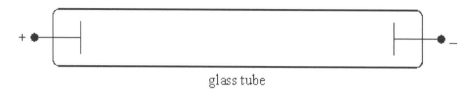

glass tube

(i) Explain why light was emitted.

(ii) State why the glow was not observed until the pressure of the air in the tube was low enough.

Q3.
In an experiment to measure the charge on a charged oil droplet, a droplet was observed between two horizontal metal plates, as shown in the diagram below, spaced 6.0 mm apart.

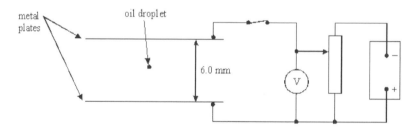

(a) The oil droplet was held stationary when a negative potential of 320 V was applied to the top plate, keeping the lower plate at zero potential.

(i) State the sign of the charge on the droplet.

(ii) With reference to the forces acting on the droplet explain why it was stationary.

(b) The potential difference between the plates was then switched off and the droplet fell at constant speed through a vertical distance of 1.20 mm in 13.8 s.
(i) Calculate its speed of descent.

(ii) By considering the forces on the spherical droplet of radius r as it falls at constant speed v, show that

$$v = \frac{2\rho g r^2}{9\eta}$$

where η is the viscosity of the air between the plates and ρ is the density of the oil. Ignore buoyancy effects.

(iii) Calculate the radius of the droplet and hence show that its mass is 2.6×10^{-15} kg.

viscosity of the air $= 1.8 \times 10^{-5}$ N s m^{-2}
density of the oil $= 960$ kg m^{-3}

(iv) Calculate the charge carried by this droplet.

Q4.
(a) An electron beam enters a uniform magnetic field and leaves at right angles, as shown in the diagram which is drawn to full-scale.

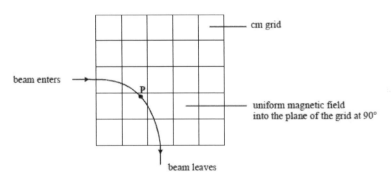

(i) Draw an arrow at P to show the direction of the force on an electron in the beam.

(ii) Explain why the kinetic energy of the electrons in the beam is constant.

(b) (i) Measure the radius of curvature of the electron beam in the diagram

(ii) The electron beam was produced by means of an electron gun in which each electron was accelerated through a potential difference of 3.2 kV. The magnetic flux density was 7.6 mT. Use these data and your measured value of the radius of curvature of the electron beam to determine the specific charge of the electron, e/m.

Q5.
In an experiment (first done by Millikan) to determine the charge on an electron, a charged oil drop of known (pre-determined) mass is held stationary between two parallel plates where a uniform electric field strength exists. Figure 1 shows this situation for one oil drop.

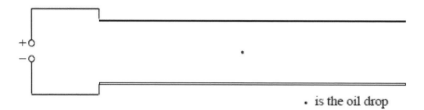

. is the oil drop

Figure 1

(a) (i) Explain what is meant by *a uniform electric field strength*.

(ii) Sketch, on **Figure 1**, electric field lines to represent the electric field between and at the edges of the plates.

(b) In one test an oil drop has a weight of 3.0×10^{-14} N. It is held stationary between plates 4.0 mm apart when the potential difference applied is 380 V.
(i) Calculate the electric field strength between the plates.

(ii) Calculate the magnitude of the charge on the oil drop.
(iii) State and explain whether the charge is positive or negative.

(c) The oil drop is not isolated but has other charged oil drops nearby. Suppose that there is another drop which has an equal but opposite charge near to the drop being observed, as shown in **Figure 2**.

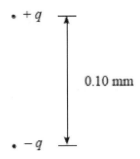

Figure 2

Show that, when the two drops are separated by 0.10 mm, the magnitude of the electric force between these oil drops may be neglected in the calculations in part (b).

The permittivity of free space, $\varepsilon_0 = 8.9 \times 10^{-12}$ F m^{-1}

Q6.
A charged oil droplet of mass 7.3×10^{-15} kg was observed between two oppositely charged horizontal metal plates, as shown in the diagram. The plates were at a fixed spacing of 5.0 mm.

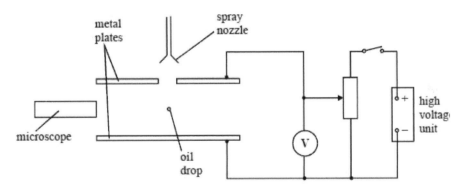

The droplet was held stationary when the plate p. d. was switched on and adjusted so that the top plate was at a potential of +750 V relative to the lower plate.

(a) Calculate the charge of the droplet.

(b) Similar measurements by Millikan proved that the charge of an oil droplet is always a whole number times 1.6×10^{-19} C. What was the significance of this discovery?

Q7.
Millikan determined the charge on individual oil droplets using an arrangement as represented in the diagram. The plate voltage necessary to hold a charged droplet stationary was measured. The time the droplet took to fall a known distance with the plate voltage off was then measured.

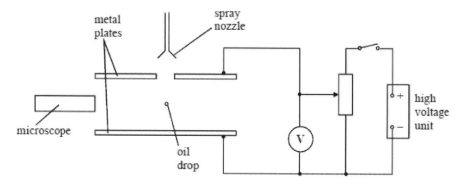

(a) (i) Explain why a charged oil droplet reaches a constant speed when the plate voltage is switched off.

(ii) By considering the forces on such a droplet, show that the radius, r, of the droplet is related to the speed, v by

$$r^2 = \frac{9\eta v}{2\rho g}$$

where η is the viscosity of air and ρ is the density of the oil. Ignore the effects of buoyancy.

(b) In an experiment to measure the charge on an oil droplet, a charged droplet was held stationary by a voltage of 225 V between two plates at a separation of 5.0 mm. When the plate voltage was switched off, the droplet descended a vertical distance of 1.20 mm in a time of 15.5 s.
Ignore the effect of buoyancy of the air.
density of oil = 950 kg m^{-3}
viscosity of air = 1.8×10^{-5} N s m^{-2}

100

(i) Show that the mass of this droplet was 2.2×10^{-15} kg.

(ii) Calculate the charge carried by this droplet.

(c) Millikan measured the charge on each of many oil droplets. Explain what he concluded from his measurements.

Q8.
(a) In a cathode ray tube, electrons emitted from a cathode are attracted towards an anode by means of a large potential difference. If the anode-cathode potential difference is 2200 V, calculate the kinetic energy, in J, and speed of each electron just before impact at the anode.

(b) (i) If an electron of this energy was to impinge on a fluorescent screen, calculate the shortest wavelength of the electromagnetic radiation subsequently emitted and explain why this is a minimum value.

(ii) Calculate the de Broglie wavelength of an electron with the same energy as that hitting the screen previously.

Q9.
(a) The diagram shows a narrow beam of electrons produced by attracting electrons emitted from a filament wire to a metal plate which has a small hole in it.

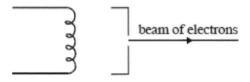
beam of electrons

(i) Why does an electric current through the filament wire cause the wire to emit electrons?

(ii) Why must the filament wire and the metal plate be in an evacuated tube?

(b) The voltage between the filament wire and the plate is 3600 V. For each electron emerging through the hole in the plate, calculate

(i) the kinetic energy, in J,

101

(ii) the speed.

Q10.
In an experiment to determine the charge on a charged oil droplet, the droplet was held stationary in a vertical electric field of strength 57 k V m^{-1}. After the electric field was switched off, the droplet fell at a steady speed, taking 18.3 s to fall through a vertical distance of 2.0 mm.

viscosity of air = 1.8×10^{-5} N s m^{-2},
density of the oil = 970 kg m^{-3}.

(a) Calculate the speed of the droplet when it was falling.
(b) Show that the droplet's radius was 9.7×10^{-7} m.
(c) Calculate the charge of the droplet.

Q11.
A charged oil droplet of mass 46×10^{-16} kg is observed between two horizontal metal plates spaced 40 mm apart.

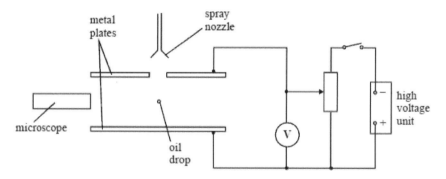

(a) The droplet is held stationary with the top plate at a potential of -565 V relative to the lower plate.

(i) What is the sign of the charge carried by the droplet?

(ii) Calculate the magnitude of the charge on the droplet. Ignore buoyancy effects

(iii) Comment on the significance of this result

(b) State and explain the direction in which the droplet would move if the top plate were made more negative relative to the lower plate.

Q12.
Figure 1 shows an electron gun that produces electrons with a kinetic energy of 6.0×10^{-16} J.

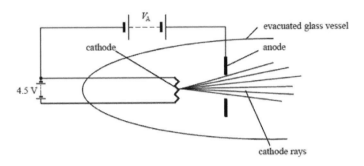

Figure 1

(a) (i) Calculate the cathode-anode potential, V_A.

(ii) What part does the 4.5 V power supply play in producing electrons?

(b) After leaving an electron gun, a narrow beam of electrons of speed 3.6 $\times 10^7$ m s^{-1} enters a uniform electric field at right angles to the field. The electric field is due to two oppositely charged parallel plates of length 60 mm, separated by a distance of 25 mm as shown in **Figure 2**. The potential difference between the plates is adjusted to 1250 V so that the beam just emerges from the field at P without touching the positive plate.

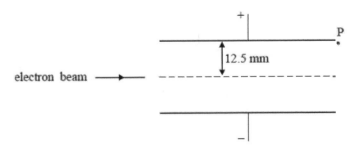

Figure 2
(i) On **Figure 2**, sketch the path of the beam in the field and beyond.

103

(ii) Calculate the time for which each electron is between the plates.

(iii) Use the data above to calculate the specific charge of the electron, e/m.

Q13.
(a) A beam of monoenergetic electrons is produced by *thermionic emission* from a metal filament, using an arrangement represented in the diagram.

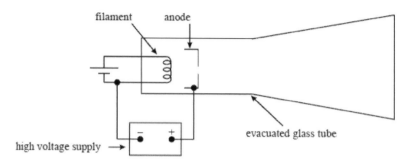

(i) Describe the process of thermionic emission.

(ii) Explain why thermionic emission is negligible when the filament current is too low.

(b) The anode is at a positive potential of 4200 V with respect to the filament.

(i) Calculate the kinetic energy, in J, of an electron in the beam in part (a) as it passes through the anode.

(ii) Calculate the speed of the electrons in this beam as they pass through the anode. Ignore relativistic effects.

Q14.
A narrow beam of electrons is produced in a vacuum tube using the arrangement shown in Figure1.

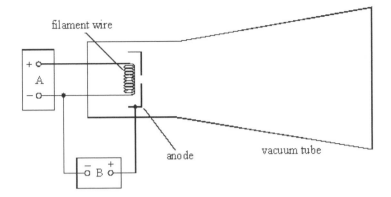

filament wire

A

anode   vacuum tube

B

Figure 1

(a) Describe the function of each voltage supply unit and state a typical voltage for each unit.

(i) unit A

(ii) unit B

(b) State and explain the effect on the beam of

(i) reducing the voltage of A,

(ii) increasing the voltage of B.

Q15.
In an experiment to measure the charge of an oil droplet, a positively charged oil droplet was held stationary by means of a uniform electric field of strength 4.9×10^5 Vm^{-1}.

(a) (i) What was the direction of the electric field?

(ii) Show that the specific charge of the oil droplet was 2.0×10^{-5} C kg^{-1}.

(b) When the electric field was switched off the oil droplet fell and quickly reached constant speed.

Explain why the oil droplet reached constant speed.

Q16.
Electrons are emitted by the process of *thermionic emission* from a metal wire in an *evacuated* container. The electrons are attracted to a metal anode which has a small hole at its centre. The anode is at a fixed *positive potential* relative to the wire. A beam of electrons emerges through the hole at constant velocity.

(a) Explain

(i) what is meant by thermionic emission,

(ii) why it is essential that the container is evacuated,

(iii) why the anode must be at a positive potential.

(b) An electron is accelerated from rest through a potential difference of 2500 V between the wire and the anode.
Calculate

(i) the kinetic energy of the electron at the anode,

(ii) the speed of the electron at the anode. Ignore relativistic effects.

Q17.
The diagram shows a narrow beam of electrons directed at right angles into a uniform electric field between two oppositely-charged parallel metal plates at a fixed potential difference.

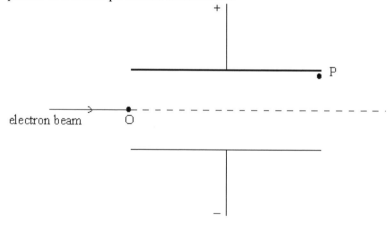

(a) The electrons enter the field at O and leave it at P. Sketch the path of the beam from O to P and beyond P.

(b) A uniform magnetic field is applied to the beam perpendicular to the electric field and to the direction of the beam. The magnetic field reduces the deflection of the beam from its initial direction.

(i) Explain why the magnetic field has this effect on the beam.
(ii) The magnetic flux density is adjusted until the beam passes through the two fields without deflection. Show that the speed v of the electrons when this occurs is given by

$$v = \frac{E}{B}$$

where E is the electric field strength and B is the magnetic flux density.

(c) In an experiment to measure the specific charge of the electron, electrons were accelerated from rest through a potential difference of 2900 V to a speed of 3.2×10^7 m s^{-1}. Use this information to calculate the specific charge of the electron.

Q18.
A charged oil droplet was observed falling between two oppositely charged parallel plates, as shown in Figure 1.

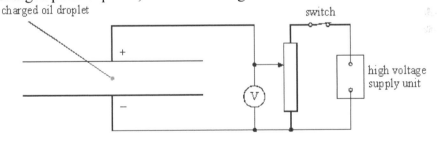

Figure 1

(a) Explain why the droplet stopped moving and remained stationary when the potential difference between the plates was adjusted to a certain value, V_c.

(b) (i) The spacing between the plates is 6.0 mm. A charged oil droplet of mass 6.2×10^{-14} kg is stopped when $V_c = 5700$ V. Calculate the charge on this droplet.

(ii) Describe and explain what would have happened to this droplet if the potential difference had been greater than 5700 V.

Q19.
In an experiment to measure the charge of the electron, a charged oil droplet of unknown mass was observed between two horizontal parallel metal plates, as shown in the figure below.

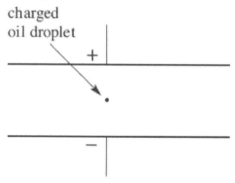

(a) The droplet was observed falling vertically at its terminal speed when the pd between the plates was zero.

(i) By considering the forces acting on the droplet as it falls at its terminal velocity, v, show that the radius, r, of the droplet is given by

$$r = \left(\frac{9\eta v}{2\rho g}\right)^{\frac{1}{2}}$$

where η is the viscosity of air and ρ is the density of the oil droplet.

(ii) Explain how the mass of the oil droplet can be determined from its radius, r.

(b) (i) The two horizontal parallel metal plates were 5.0 mm apart. The mass of the droplet was 6.8×10^{-15} kg. The droplet was held stationary when the plate pd was 690 V.

Calculate the charge of the oil droplet, expressing your answer to an appropriate number of significant figures.

(ii) Millikan made the first accurate measurements of the charge carried by charged oil droplets. Outline what Millikan concluded from these measurements.

Q20.
The figure below shows an electron gun in an evacuated tube. Electrons emitted by *thermionic emission* from the metal filament are attracted to the metal anode which is at a fixed potential, V, relative to the filament. Some of the electrons pass though a small hole in the anode to form a beam which is directed into a uniform magnetic field.

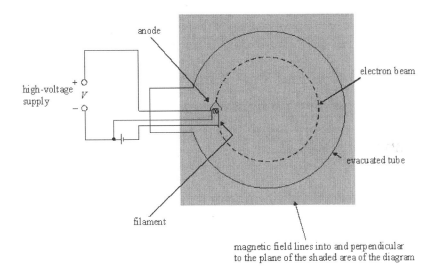

magnetic field lines into and perpendicular to the plane of the shaded area of the diagram

(a) (i) Explain what is meant by thermionic emission.

(ii) Show that the speed, v, of the electrons in the beam is given by

$$v = \left(\frac{2eV}{m}\right)^{\frac{1}{2}}$$

where m is the mass of the electron and e is the charge of the electron.

(b) The beam of electrons travels through the field in a circular path at constant speed.

(i) Explain why the electrons travel at constant speed in the magnetic field.

(ii) Show that the radius, r, of the circular path of the beam in the field is given by

$$r = \left(\frac{2mV}{B^2e}\right)^{\frac{1}{2}}$$

where B is the magnetic flux density and V is the pd between the anode and the filament.

(iii) The arrangement described above was used to measure the specific charge of the electron, e/m. Use the following data to calculate e/m.
$B = 3.1$ mT $r = 25$ mm $V = 530$ V

Q21.
A narrow beam of electrons is produced in a vacuum tube using an electron gun, part of which is shown in Figure 1.

Figure 1

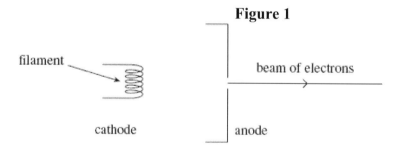

(a) (i) State and explain the effect on the beam of electrons of increasing the filament current.

(ii) State and explain the effect on the beam of electrons of increasing the anode potential.

(b) The beam of electrons is directed at right angles into a uniform magnetic field as shown in **Figure 2**.

Figure 2

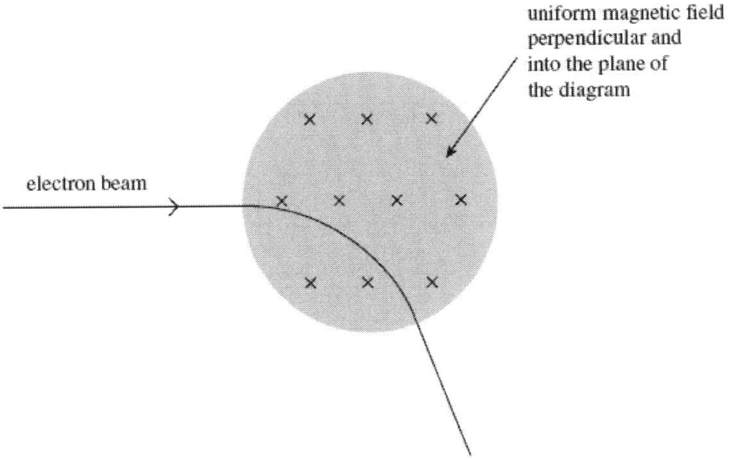

uniform magnetic field
perpendicular and
into the plane of
the diagram

electron beam

(i) Explain why the electrons move in a circular path at a constant speed in the magnetic field.

(ii) When the speed of the electrons in the beam is 7.4×10^6 m s^{-1} and the magnetic flux density is 0.60 m T, the radius of curvature of the beam is 68 mm.

Use these data to calculate the specific charge of the electron, stating an appropriate unit. Give your answer to an appropriate number of significant figures.

(iii) Discuss the historical relevance of the value of the specific charge of the electron compared with the specific charge of the H$^+$ ion.

Q22.
The diagram shows apparatus which can be used to determine the specific charge of an electron.

111

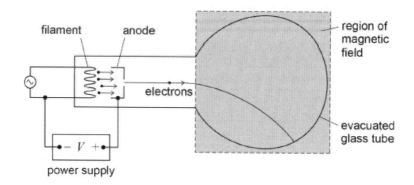

Electrons are emitted from the filament and accelerated by a potential difference between the filament and anode to produce a beam. The beam is deflected into a circular path by applying a magnetic field perpendicular to the plane of the diagram.

(a) Describe the process that releases the electrons emitted at the filament.

(b) The table shows the data collected when determining the specific charge of the electron by the method shown in the diagram.

potential difference V that accelerates the electrons	320 V
radius r of circular path of the electrons in the magnetic field	4.0 cm
flux density B of the applied magnetic field	1.5 mT

Show that the specific charge of the electron is given by the expression

$$\frac{2V}{B^2 r^2}$$

(c) Using data from the table, calculate a value for the specific charge of the electron.

Give your answer to an appropriate number of significant figures.

(d) At the time when Thomson measured the specific charge of the particles in cathode rays, the largest specific charge known was that of the hydrogen ion.

State how Thomson's result for the specific charge of each particle within a cathode ray compared with that for the hydrogen ion and explain what he concluded about the nature of the particles.

Q23.
A narrow beam of electrons is directed into the region between two parallel plates, P and Q. When a constant potential difference is applied between the two plates, the beam curves downwards towards plate Q as shown in the figure below.

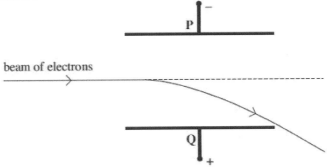

(a) Explain why the beam curves downwards at an increasing angle to its initial direction.

(b) A uniform magnetic field is then applied at right angles to both the beam and the electric field between the plates **P** and **Q**. As a result, the downward deflection of the beam is increased.

(i) The arrangement is to be used to determine the speed of the electrons in the beam. Describe what adjustments to the flux density B of the magnetic field should be made to reduce the deflection of the beam to zero.

(ii) Explain why the electrons pass undeflected through the fields when their speed v is given by

$$v = \frac{V}{Bd}$$

where V is the potential difference between plates **P** and **Q** and d is the perpendicular distance between the plates.

(c) The beam of electrons was produced by thermionic emission from a heated filament. When the potential difference between the anode and the filament was 4200 V, the speed of the electrons in the beam was 3.9×10^7 ms^{-1}.

Use this information to determine the specific charge of the electron.

Q24.
A charged oil droplet was observed between two horizontal metal plates X and Y, as shown in the diagram below.

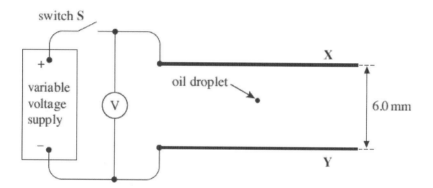

(a) (i) With the switch **S** open, the droplet fell vertically at a constant velocity of 1.1×10^{-4} ms^{-1}. Show that the radius of the droplet is about 1.0×10^{-6} m. Assume the droplet is spherical.

density of oil, $\rho = 880$ kg m^{-3} viscosity of air, $\eta = 1.8 \times 10^{-5}$ N s m^{-2}

(ii) Calculate the mass of the droplet.

(iii) The switch **S** was closed and the potential difference from the voltage supply was adjusted gradually to reduce the downward motion of the droplet. The droplet stopped moving when the potential difference across the plates was 680 V. The spacing between the plates was 6.0 mm. Calculate the magnitude of the charge on the droplet.

(b) The mass of another charged droplet was found to be 4.3×10^{-15} kg. With switch **S** closed and the voltage supply at its maximum value of 1000 V, this droplet fell more slowly than when the switch was open but it could not be stopped.

Explain why this droplet could not be held at rest and show that the magnitude of the charge on it was 1.6×10^{-19} C.

Q25.
The following figure shows a discharge tube containing a gas at low pressure. When a sufficiently high potential difference is applied between the two electrodes in the tube the gas becomes conducting and emits light.

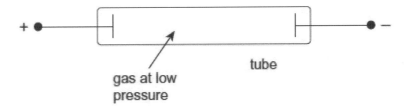

(a) (i) Describe how the charged particles responsible for conduction in the gas are produced.

(ii) Explain why the gas emits light and why it must be at low pressure.

(b) The charged particles moving towards the negative electrode were initially referred to as positive rays. Explain why their **specific charge** depends on the choice of gas in the tube.

Q26.
The diagram below shows part of an evacuated tube that is used to determine the specific charge (e / m) for an electron. An electron beam is directed between the two parallel metal plates, X and Y. In the region between the plates, a magnetic field is applied perpendicularly into the plane of the diagram. An electric field can be applied in this region by applying a potential difference (pd) between the plates.

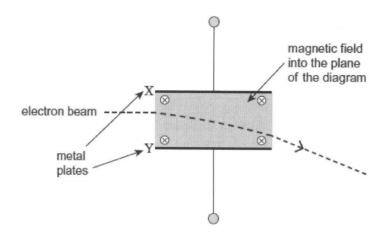

(a) The diagram shows the path of the electron beam when the magnetic field is applied and the pd between X and Y is zero.

(i) Explain why the path followed by the electron beam in the magnetic field is a circular arc.

(ii) Show that the speed v of the electrons is given by $v = \dfrac{Ber}{m}$
where r is the radius of the path of an electron in the magnetic field and B is the flux density of the magnetic field.

(iii) A pd V is now applied between X and Y without changing the flux density of the magnetic field. V is adjusted until the electron beam is not deflected as it travels in the region between the plates.

Determine an expression for the speed v of the electrons in terms of V, B and the separation d of the metal plates.

(b) Use the equation given in part (ii) and your answer to part (iii) to show that the specific charge for the electron $= \dfrac{V}{B^2 rd}$

(c) If the charge on an electron is known then its mass can be determined from the specific charge. Describe how Millikan's experiment with charged oil droplets enables the electronic charge to be determined. Include in your answer:

- the procedures used to determine the radius of a droplet and the charge on a droplet
- how the measurements made are used
- how the electronic charge can be deduced.

The quality of your written communication will be assessed in your answer.

Q27.
The diagram shows a vacuum photocell in which a metal surface is illuminated by electromagnetic radiation of a single wavelength. Electrons emitted from the metal surface are collected by terminal T in the photocell. This results in a photocurrent, I, which is measured by the microammeter.

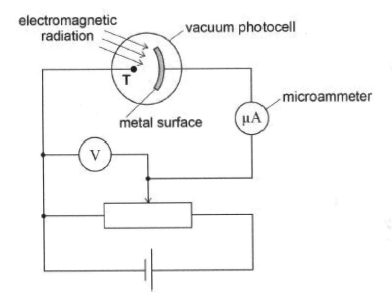

The potential divider is adjusted until the photocurrent is zero.
The potential difference shown on the voltmeter is 0.50 V
The work function of the metal surface is 6.2 eV

(a) Calculate the wavelength, in nm, of the electromagnetic radiation incident on the metal surface.

(b) The intensity of the electromagnetic radiation is increased. No adjustment is made to the potential divider.

The classical wave model and the photon model make different predictions about the effect on the photocurrent.

Explain the effect on the photocurrent that each model predicts and how experimental observations confirm the photon model.

(c) The potential divider in the diagram is returned to its original position so that a photocurrent is detected by the microammeter.

The potential divider is then adjusted to increase the potential difference shown on the voltmeter.

Explain why the photocurrent decreases when this adjustment to the potential divider is made.

(d) The apparatus shown in the diagram above is used to investigate three different metal surfaces **A**, **B** and **C**.

The table shows, for each of the three surfaces, a voltmeter reading V and the corresponding photocurrent I. The same source of electromagnetic radiation is used throughout the investigation.

	V/V	$I/\mu A$
Metal surface **A**	1.5	56
Metal surface **B**	2.5	56
Metal surface **C**	2.5	78

Which conclusion about the relationship between the work functions of **A**, **B** and **C** is correct?

Tick (✔) the correct box.

A > B > C. ☐

A < B < C.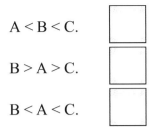

B > A > C.

B < A < C.

Q28.

Figure 1 shows a narrow beam of electrons produced by attracting the electrons emitted from a filament wire, to a positively charged metal plate which has a small hole in it.

Figure 1

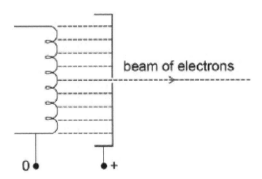

(a) Explain why an electric current through the filament wire causes the wire to emit electrons.

(b) Explain why the filament wire and the metal plates must be in an evacuated tube.

(c) The potential difference between the filament wire and the metal plate is 4800 V.

Calculate the de Broglie wavelength of the electrons in the beam.

The beam is directed at a thin metal foil between the metal plate and a fluorescent screen at the end of the tube, as shown in **Figure 2**. The electrons that pass through the metal foil cause a pattern of concentric rings on the screen.

Figure 2

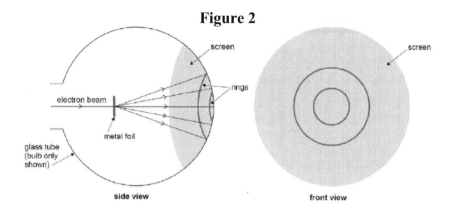

side view   front view

(d) The potential difference between the filament and the metal plate is increased. State and explain the effect this has on the diameter of the rings.

Q29.
The diagram shows a gas discharge tube devised by William Crookes in one of his investigations.

When a large potential difference is applied between the cathode and anode the paddle wheel is seen to rotate and travel along the rail towards the anode.

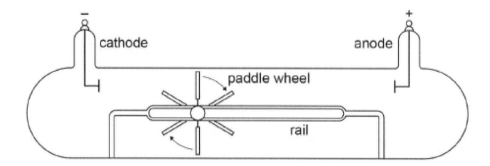

(a) Explain how this experiment led Crookes to conclude that cathode rays are particles and that these particles caused the movement of the paddle.

(b) Later experiments showed that cathode rays are electrons in motion. Explain how cathode rays are produced in a gas discharge tube.

120

(c) In a particular gas discharge tube, air molecules inside the tube are absorbed by the walls of the tube.
Suggest the effect that this absorption may have on the motion of the paddle wheel.

Give a reason for your answer.

Q30.
In an experiment to measure the charge of the electron, a spherical charged oil droplet of unknown mass is observed between two horizontal parallel metal plates, as shown in the diagram below.

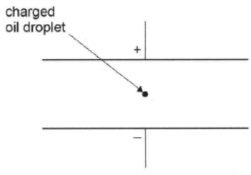

(a) The droplet falls vertically at its terminal speed when the potential difference (pd) between the plates is zero.

A droplet of radius r falls at its terminal velocity, v.
Derive an expression for r in terms of v, η , ρ and g, where η is the viscosity of air and ρ is the density of the oil droplet.

(b) Explain how the mass of the oil droplet can be calculated from its radius and other relevant data.

(c) A potential difference (pd) is applied across the plates and is adjusted until the droplet is held stationary. The two horizontal parallel metal plates are 15.0 mm apart. The mass of the droplet is 3.4×10^{-15} kg.

The droplet is held stationary when the pd across the plates is 1560 V.
Calculate the charge of the oil droplet.

(d) A student carries out Millikan's oil drop experiment and obtains the following results for the charges on the oil drops that were investigated.

-9.6×10^{-19} C -12.8×10^{-19} C -6.4×10^{-19} C

Discuss the extent to which the student's results support Millikan's conclusion and how the student's conclusion should be different.

Q31.
The diagram below shows part of an apparatus used to determine the specific charge of an electron.

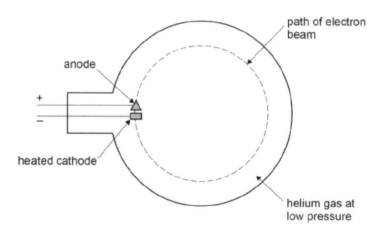

Electrons are emitted by the cathode by thermionic emission. They are accelerated by the potential difference between the cathode and anode.

The tube contains helium gas at a low pressure and the gas emits light to show the path of the electron beam.

The beam is bent into a circular path by applying a magnetic field perpendicular to the plane of the diagram.

(a) Explain how light is emitted as the electrons travel through the helium gas.

(b) In one experiment the potential difference between the cathode and anode is 2.5 kV.

Show that the speed of the electrons is about 3.0×10^7 m s^{-1}.

(c) When the flux density of the magnetic field is 3.1 mT the diameter of the path of the beam is 0.114 m.

Calculate the value for the specific charge of an electron from the data in this experiment.

(d) In practice the path of the electron beam is not a perfect circle. Discuss how the presence of the gas affects the path of the electrons.

Q32.
The diagram shows the main parts of a transmission electron microscope (TEM).

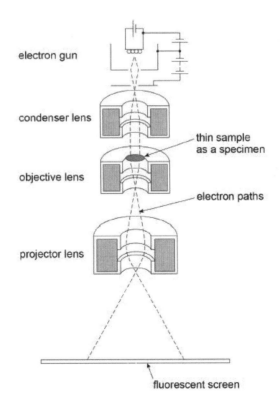

electron gun

condenser lens

thin sample as a specimen

objective lens

electron paths

projector lens

fluorescent screen

(a) What is the process by which electrons are produced in an electron gun?
Tick (✔) the correct box.

Beta particle emission ☐

Electron diffraction ☐

Photoelectric effect ☐

Thermionic emission ☐

(b) The electrons in a particular TEM have a kinetic energy of 4.1×10^{-16} J.
Relativistic effects are negligible for this electron energy.

Suggest, with a calculation, whether the images of individual atoms can, in principle, be resolved in this TEM.

(c) A typical TEM can accelerate electrons to very high speeds and form high resolution images.

Explain:
•the process of image formation, and
•the factors that affect the quality of, and the level of detail in, the image.

Q33.
(a) J J Thomson devised the first experiments to determine the specific charge for cathode rays produced in discharge tubes. He found that the value did not depend on the gas in the tube. He also discovered that particles emitted by a heated filament and particles emitted in the photoelectric effect had the same specific charge.

State two conclusions that were drawn from Thomson's experiments.

(b) The diagram shows a spherical tube, filled with low-pressure helium gas, that is used in an experiment to determine the specific charge of an electron.

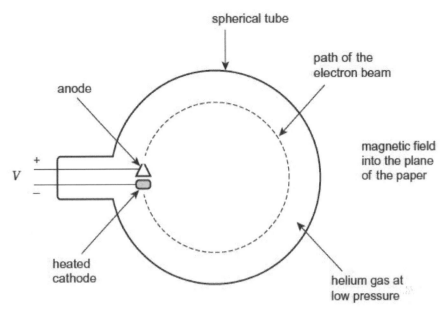

spherical tube

path of the
electron beam

anode

V

+

−

magnetic field
into the plane
of the paper

heated
cathode

helium gas at
low pressure

Electrons are accelerated by a potential difference (pd) V applied between the cathode and anode. A magnetic field of known flux density B, directed into the plane of the diagram, causes the electrons to move in a circular path.

(i) Explain the process that causes the low-pressure helium gas to emit light so that the path of the electron beam can be seen.

(ii) In one experiment using the apparatus in the diagram, the accelerating pd is 1.6 kV and the flux density of the magnetic field is 2.2 mT. The path of the electron beam has a radius of 0.059 m.
Determine a value for the specific charge of an electron using these data.
State an appropriate unit for your answer.

Relativity

Q1.
Figure 1 shows a diagram of the Michelson-Morley interferometer that was used to try to detect the absolute motion of the Earth through the ether (æther).

Light from the monochromatic source passes through the semi-silvered glass block and takes two different paths to the viewing telescope. The two paths, PM_1 and PM_2, are the same length. Interference fringes are observed through the viewing telescope.

Figure 1

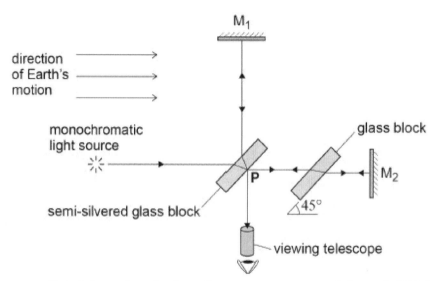

It was predicted that when the interferometer was rotated through 90° the fringe pattern would shift by 0.4 of the fringe spacing.

(a) Explain how the experiment provided a means of testing the idea that the Earth had an absolute motion relative to the aether.
Your answer should include:
• an explanation of why a shift of the fringe pattern was predicted
• a comparison of the results of the experiment to the prediction
• the conclusion about the Earth's absolute motion through the aether.

126

(b) The Michelson-Morley experiment provides evidence for one of the postulates of Einstein's theory of special relativity. State this postulate.

(c) State the other postulate of Einstein's theory of special relativity.

(d) One consequence of the special theory of relativity is length contraction.

Experimental evidence for length contraction is provided by the decay of muons produced in the atmosphere by cosmic rays.

Figure 2 shows how the percentage of the number of muons remaining in a sample changes with time as measured by an observer in a frame of reference that is stationary relative to the muons.

Figure 2

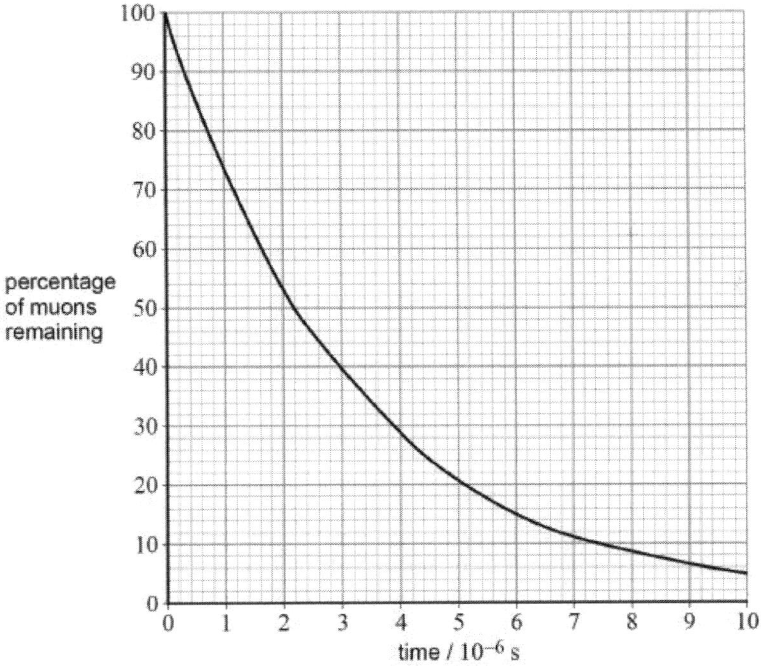

percentage of muons remaining

time / 10^{-6} s

In a particular experiment, muons moving with a velocity $0.990c$ travel a distance of 1310 m through the atmosphere to a detector.

Determine the percentage of muons that reach the detector.

127

Q2.
(a) One of the two postulates of Einstein's theory of special relativity is that the speed of light in free space is invariant.

(i) Explain what is meant by this statement.

(ii) What is the other postulate?

(b) K^+ mesons are sub-atomic particles of half-life 86 ns when at rest. In an accelerator experiment, a beam of K^+ mesons travelling at a speed of $0.95c$ is created, where c is the speed of light.

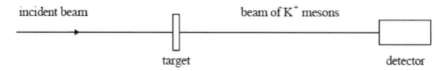

incident beam   beam of K^+ mesons

target   detector

(i) Calculate the half-life of the K^+ mesons in the beam measured in the laboratory frame of reference.

(ii) What is the greatest distance that a detector could be sited from the point of production of the K^+ mesons to detect at least 25% of the K^+ mesons produced?

Q3.
(a) Michelson and Morley attempted to detect absolute motion by investigating whether or not the speed of light in a direction parallel to the Earth's motion differs from the speed of light perpendicular to the Earth's motion.
Discuss what resulted from this experiment and what was concluded.

(b) In a science fiction story, a space rocket left the Earth in 2066 and travelled out of the Solar System at a speed of $0.80c$, where c is the speed of light in vacuo, to a star 16 light years from the Earth.

(i) How many years, in the frame of reference of the Earth, did the spacecraft take to reach the star?

(ii)What was the distance, in the frame of reference of the spacecraft, between the Earth and the star?

(iii) A member of the crew was 21 years old on leaving the Earth. How old was this person on arrival at the star?

Q4.
The diagram represents the Michelson-Morley interferometer.

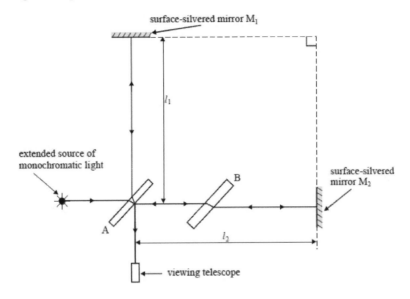

surface-silvered mirror M₁

extended source of monochromatic light

surface-silvered mirror M₂

viewing telescope

(a) (i) Name the object labelled A.

(ii) Name the object labelled B and explain its purpose.

(b) Describe and explain what is observed through the viewing telescope

(i) when distances l_1 and l_2 are equal.

(ii) as distance l_1 is made slightly longer than distance l_2.

(c) Michelson and Morley used the interferometer to try to detect the motion of the Earth through the hypothetical aether.

(i) Outline how the apparatus was used and state what the result was.

(ii) Explain the significance of the result.

Q5.
In a particle beam experiment, a pulsed beam of protons at a speed of 1.00 $\times 10^8$ m s^{-1} passed through a stationary detector in a time of 15.0 ns.

beam of protons

detector

(a) Calculate the length of the pulsed beam in

(i) the frame of reference of the detector,

(ii) the frame of reference of the protons.

(b) (i)Calculate the kinetic energy of each proton in the beam, in J.

(ii) The beam consisted of 10^7 protons. It passed through the detector and was stopped by a stationary target. Calculate the average power which the proton beam delivered to the target during the pulse.

Q6.
(a) In a particle beam experiment, a short pulse of 1 ns duration of particles moving at constant speed passed directly between 2 detectors at a fixed distance apart of 240 m.

The pulse took 0.84 μs to travel from one detector to the other.

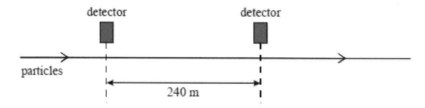

detector   detector

particles

240 m

(i) Calculate the speed of the particles.

(ii) Calculate the distance between the two detectors in the frame of reference of the particles.

(b) In a 'thought experiment' about relativity, a student stated that a twin who travelled from the Earth to a distant planet and back at a speed close to the speed of light would be the same age on return as the twin who stayed on Earth. Explain why this statement is **not** correct.

Q7.
(a) One of the two postulates of Einstein's theory of special relativity is that the speed of light in free space is invariant.

(i) Explain what is meant by this postulate.

(ii) State and explain the other postulate.

(b) A stationary muon has a rest mass of 1.88×10^{-28} kg and a half-life of 2.2×10^{-6} s.

Calculate

(i) the mass of a muon travelling at $0.996\, c$, where c is the speed of light in a vacuum,

(ii) the distance, in a laboratory frame of reference, travelled in one half-life by a muon moving at $0.996\, c$.

Q8.
(a) The speed of an object cannot be greater than or equal to the speed of light yet its kinetic energy can be increased without limit. Explain the apparent contradiction that the speed of an object is limited whereas its kinetic energy is not limited.

(b) Protons are accelerated from rest through a potential difference of 2.1×10^{10} V.

(i) Show that the kinetic energy of a proton after it has been accelerated from rest through this potential difference is 3.4×10^{-9} J.

(ii) Show that the mass of a proton with the kinetic energy value calculated in part (a) is approximately $23 m_0$, where m_0 is its rest mass.

(c) Calculate the speed of a proton which has a mass equal to $23 m_0$.

131

Q9.

The Michelson-Morley experiment represented in the diagram was designed to find out if the speed of light depended on its direction relative to the Earth's motion through space. Interference fringes were seen by the observer.

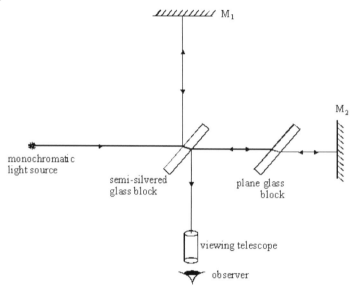

(a) (i) Explain why interference fringes were seen.

(ii) The interference fringe pattern did not shift when the apparatus was rotated by 90°. Explain the significance of this null observation.

(b) Einstein postulated that the speed of light in free space is invariant. Explain what is meant by this postulate.

Q10.
(i) Calculate the kinetic energy, in J, of a proton accelerated in a straight line from rest through a potential difference of 1.1×10^9 V.

(ii) Show that the mass of a proton at this energy is 2.2 m_0, where m_0 is the proton rest mass.

(iii) Hence calculate the speed of a proton of mass 2.2 m_0.

Q11.
(a) One of the two postulates of Einstein's theory of special relativity is that *physical laws have the same form in all inertial frames of reference.*

Explain, with the aid of a suitable example, what is meant by an inertial frame of reference.

(b) A certain type of sub-atomic particle has a half-life of 18 ns when at rest. A beam of these particles travelling at a speed of 0.995c is produced in an accelerator.

(i) Calculate the half-life of these particles in the laboratory frame of reference.

(ii) Calculate the time taken by these particles to travel a distance of 108 m in the laboratory at a speed of 0.995c and hence show that the intensity of the beam is reduced to 25% of its original value over this distance.

Q12.
(a) In a science fiction film, a space rocket travels away from the Earth at a speed of 0.994 c, where c is the speed of light in free space. A radio message of duration 800 s is transmitted by the space rocket.

(i) Calculate the duration of the message when it is received at the Earth.

(ii) Calculate the distance moved by the rocket in the Earth's frame of reference in the time taken to send the message.

(b) A student claims that a twin who travels at a speed close to the speed of light from Earth to a distant star and back would, on return to Earth, be a different age to the twin who stayed on Earth. Discuss whether or not this claim is correct.

Q13.
(a) A student models a spacecraft journey that takes one year. The spacecraft travels directly away from an observer at a speed of 1.2×10^7 m s^{-1}. The student predicts that a clock stationary relative to the observer will record a time several days longer than an identical clock on the spacecraft.

Comment on the student's prediction. Support your answer with a time dilation calculation.

(b) In practice, the gravitational field of the Sun affects the motion of the spacecraft and it does not travel directly away from the Earth throughout the journey.

Explain why this means that the theory of special relativity cannot be applied to the journey.

Q14.
(a) Calculate the speed at which a matter particle has a mass equal to 10 times its rest mass.

(b) Explain why a matter particle can not travel as fast as a photon in free space even though its kinetic energy can be increased without limit.

Q15.
π mesons, travelling in a straight line at a speed of 0.95 c, pass two detectors 34 m apart, as shown in the figure below.

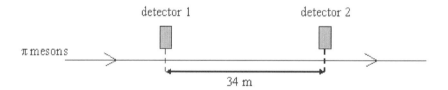

(i) Calculate the time taken, in the frame of reference of the detectors, for a π meson to travel between the two detectors.

(ii) π mesons are unstable and decay with a half-life of 18 ns when at rest. Show that approximately 75% of the π mesons passing the first detector decay before they reach the second detector.

Q16.
(a) One of the two postulates of Einstein's theory of special relativity is that the speed of light in free space, c, is invariant.
Explain what is meant by this statement.

(b) A beam of identical particles moving at a speed of $0.98c$ is directed along a straight line between two detectors 25 m apart.

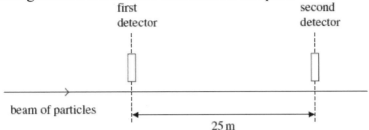

beam of particles

25 m

The particles are unstable and the intensity of the beam at the second detector is a quarter of the intensity at the first detector.
Calculate the half-life of the particles in their rest frame.

Q17.
In an experiment, a beam of protons moving along a straight line at a constant speed of $1.8 \times 10^8 ms^{-1}$ took 95 ns to travel between two detectors at a fixed distance d_0 apart, as shown in the figure below.

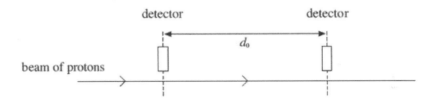

(a) (i) Calculate the distance d_0 between the two detectors in the frame of reference of the detectors.

(ii) Calculate the distance between the two detectors in the frame of reference of the protons.

(b) A proton is moving at a speed of $1.8 \times 10^8 ms^{-1}$

$$Calculate\ the\ ratio = \frac{kinetic\ energy\ of\ proton}{rest\ energy\ of\ the\ proton}$$

135

Q18.

The figure below represents the Michelson-Morley interferometer. Interference fringes are seen by an observer looking through the viewing telescope.

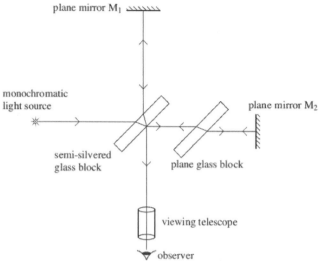

(a) Explain why the interference fringes shift their position if the distance from either of the two mirrors to the semi-silvered block is changed.

(b) Michelson and Morley predicted that the interference fringes would shift when the apparatus was rotated through 90°. When they tested their prediction, no such fringe shift was observed.

(i) Why was it predicted that a shift of the fringes would be observed?

(ii) What conclusion was drawn from the observation that the fringes did not shift?

Q19.

(a) One of the two postulates of Einstein's theory of special relativity is that physical laws have the same form in all inertial frames of reference. Explain in terms of velocity what is meant by an inertial frame of reference.

(b) Light takes 4.3 years to reach the Earth from the star Alpha Centauri.

(i) A space probe is to be sent from the Earth to the star to arrive 5.0 years later, according to an observer on Earth.

Assuming the space probe's velocity is constant, calculate its speed in ms^{-1} on this journey.

(ii) Calculate the time taken for this journey in years registered by a clock in the space probe.

Q20.
(a) Calculate the speed of a particle at which its mass is twice its rest mass.

(b) Use the axes below to show how the mass m of a particle changes from its rest mass m_o as its speed v increases from zero.

Mark and label on the graph the point **P** where the mass of the particle is twice its rest mass.

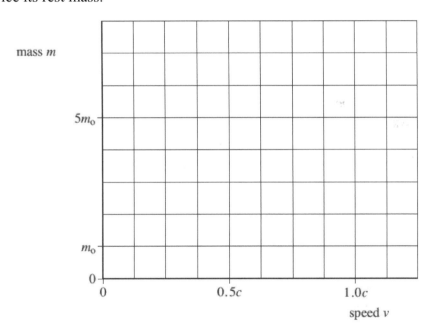

(c) By considering the relationship between the energy of a particle and its mass, explain why the theory of special relativity does not allow a matter particle to travel as fast as light.

Q21.
A muon is an unstable particle produced by cosmic rays in the Earth's atmosphere. Muons that are produced at a height of 10.7 km above the Earth's surface, travel at a speed of $0.996c$ toward Earth, where c is the speed of light. In the frame of reference of the muons, the muons have a half-life of 1.60×10^{-6} s.

(a) (i) Calculate how many muons will reach the Earth's surface for every 1000 that are produced at a height of 10.7 km.

(ii) Which of the following statements is correct? Tick ($\checkmark$) the correct answer.

	$\checkmark$ if correct
For an observer in a laboratory on Earth, the distance travelled by a muon that reaches the Earth is greater than the distance travelled by a muon in its frame of reference	
For an observer in a laboratory on Earth, time passes more slowly than it does for a muon in its frame of reference	
For an observer in a laboratory on Earth, the probability of a muon decaying each second is lower than it is for a muon in its frame of reference	

(b) (i) Show that the total energy of an electron that has been accelerated to a speed of $0.98c$ is about 4×10^{-13} J.

(2)

(ii) The total energy of an electron travelling at a speed of $0.97c$ is 3.37×10^{-13} J. Calculate the potential difference required to accelerate an electron from a speed of $0.97c$ to a speed of $0.98c$.

Q22.
The diagram shows the paths of light rays through a simplified version of the apparatus used by Michelson and Morley.

138

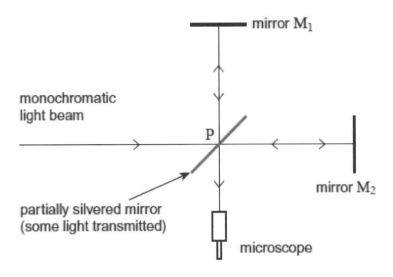

In the apparatus, light waves reflected by the mirrors M1 and M2, meet at P so that they superpose and produce interference fringes. These are observed using the microscope.

Michelson and Morley predicted that the fringes would shift when the apparatus was rotated through 90°. They thought that this shift would enable them to measure the speed of the Earth through a substance, called the aether, that was thought to fill space.

(a) Explain why Michelson and Morley expected that the fringe positions would shift when the apparatus was rotated through 90°.

(b) In their apparatus they made the distances PM_1 and PM_2 the same and equal to d. They used light of wavelength (λ) about 550 nm and knew that the speed of light c was 3.0×10^8 m s^{-1}. Using known astronomical data, they calculated the speed v at which they thought the Earth moved through the aether. They were then able to predict that when the apparatus was rotated through 90° the fringes should shift by a distance $0.4f$, where f was the fringe spacing.

(i) To determine v, Michelson and Morley assumed that the Sun was stationary with respect to the aether as the Earth moved through it. Suggest, using this assumption, how the speed v of the Earth through the aether could be determined. You do not need to do the calculation.

(ii) Michelson and Morley calculated v to be 3.0×10^4 m s^{-1}.
They worked out Δf, the magnitude of the expected shift of the fringes, using the
formula

$$\Delta f = \frac{2v^2 d}{c^2 \lambda} f$$

Calculate the distance d they used in their experiment.

(c) Although a shift of $0.4\,f$ was easily detectable, no shift was observed.
Explain what this null result demonstrated and its significance for Einstein in his special theory of relativity.

Q23.
Cosmic rays mostly consist of high-energy protons. These protons can collide with atomic nuclei in the Earth's upper atmosphere producing pions (π^-). Pions are unstable and decay into high-energy muons (μ^-).

(a) (i) Which of the following is the particle group for pions (π^-)?

Tick ($\checkmark$) the correct answer.

Baryons ☐

Leptons ☐

Mesons ☐

Photons ☐

(ii) Complete the equation for the decay of a pion (π^-).

$$\pi^- \longrightarrow \mu^- + \underline{\hspace{3cm}}$$

(b) 2.5×10^8 muons are created simultaneously above the Earth's surface.

140

These muons are unstable and have a half-life of 2.2 μs. They are created at a height of 10.7 km and travel towards the Earth's surface with a constant vertical velocity of 2.85×10^8 ms^{-1}.

(i) Show that, for the reference frame of an observer on Earth, the time taken for the muons to reach the Earth's surface is approximately 17 muon half-lives.

(ii) Estimate the number of these muons that an observer on Earth would expect to remain after 17 half-lives.

(iii) The number of muons that reach the Earth's surface is considerably different from the estimated number in part **(b)(ii)**.

Identify the theory that explains the difference between the estimated and observed number of muons.

(iv) Outline why the number of muons that actually reach the Earth's surface is different from the estimated number in part **(b)(ii)**.

(v) Calculate, for the reference frame of a muon, the time taken for the muons to travel this distance.

(vi) Calculate the number of muons that remain at the end of the time interval calculated in part **(b)(v)**.

Q24.
Cosmic rays detected on a spacecraft are protons with a total energy of 3.7 $\times 10^9$ eV.
Calculate the velocity of the protons as a fraction of the speed of light.

Q25.
(a) The theory of special relativity is based on two postulates. One of these postulates is that the speed of light in free space is invariant.
State the other postulate.

(b) An electron in the Stanford linear accelerator is accelerated to an energy of 24.0 GeV.

(i) An electron travelling with this energy has a velocity v.

Show that the value of $\left(1 - \dfrac{v^2}{c^2}\right)^{\frac{1}{2}}$ is about 2.1×10^{-5}.

(ii) The Stanford linear accelerator has a length of 3.0 km. Assume that the electron travels for the full length of the accelerator with an energy of 24 GeV.

Calculate the length, in m, of the accelerator in the reference frame of the electron.

(c) Draw a graph to show how the relativistic mass of an electron varies with speed as it is accelerated from rest.
Rest mass of an electron $= m_0$

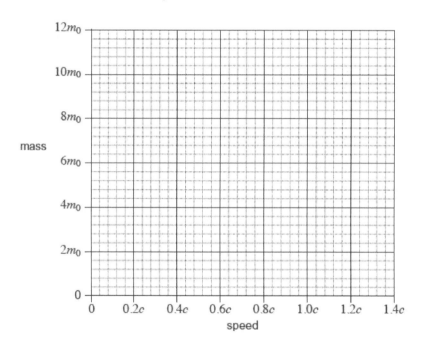

Bibliography

Atomic Physics
By Max Born

Introductiosn To Modern Physics
By John Dirk Walecka

An Introduction to Quantum Physics
By A. P. French and E.F. Taylor

Special Relativity
By A. P. French

What is Relativity
By L. D. Landau and G. B. Rumer

Introduction to the Theory of Relativity
By Peter Gabriel Bergmann

Printed in Great Britain
by Amazon

69798969R00086